Step-by-Step

*My experiences with
Marriage, Law,
Spiritual Warfare and
The Holy Spirit*

Jeffrey Sakas

Published by:

Maudlin Pond Press, LLC
PO Box 53, Tybee Island, Georgia 31328, USA

ISBN: 978-1-7356192-3-1
eBook ISBN: 978-1-7356192-4-8

Step-by-Step

A book chronicling the work of the Holy Spirit in the life of a veteran Attorney over a period of 60 years.

Jeffrey Sakas became a Christian at the age of 10, felt the presence of the Holy Spirit growing and defining His role over a significantly long period of time. After marriage, and attending law school in New Orleans, Sakas has been a practicing lawyer in Atlanta since 1973. The book is intended for an audience of believers who are uncertain of the work of the Holy Spirit in their lives and for non-believers who may not have experienced a clear calling to submit their lives to God by accepting Jesus Christ as their Lord and Savior. The book expresses both victory and failure and the certainty that we all are engaged in a spiritual war whether we are aware of that fact or not. This book is directed to those who desire the active presence of the Holy Spirit through periods of drought, conflict and loss. However, throughout the entire period of time that the book covers, the faithful presence of the Holy Spirit is evident. As an attorney the author details various complex legal matters in which he sought to bring justice to major companies on behalf poor and legally underserved individuals. As a Sunday school teacher he discusses the leadership of The Holy Sprite in understanding and applying the teachings of Jesus to his life. As a married man Sakas discusses how relationships have failed and how to overcome the problems that can happen to any individual even if he is committed to his Christian faith.

The influence of the teachings of Jesus in the "Sermon on the Mount" in Matthew 5 through 7 is of paramount importance to understand the power and the purpose of the Holy Spirit throughout the life of any Christian, including an attorney who has experienced difficulties in his relationships. The author hopes that his experience in over 60 years as a Christian and nearly 50 years as an attorney will be helpful to any individual that seeks the will of God in their life.

Table of Contents

INTRODUCTION

I originally wanted to title this book Marriage, Law, Spiritual Warfare and the Holy Spirit. My publishers decided that the book title was too long and did not lend itself to a catchy book cover. As a part of my exercise routine I go for walks. The walking is good for me and gives me time to think about who might be interested in reading this book that contains both victories and defeats in my personal life. Because I have had difficulties with my legs it is difficult for me to walk without the use of a cane. Additionally, it is painful to take steps and I have to limit the distance I walk. I think about each step that I take and have realized that Jesus also looks at each step that I take. While my concentration is on the physical limitations that define how far I can go and where I can go, the spiritual considerations by which the Holy Spirit directs my life should and must be realized as being unlimited. The realization that God directs my life through the work of the Holy Spirit is a comfort and imperative that I must accept daily. Physical steps, emotional steps and spiritual steps take us to places that make us who we are and how we want to be. This book is an examination of the steps that have occurred in my life that have brought me to where I am and where I am going. While physically limited, spiritually I am in the hands of the Almighty God and there is no limit to where He will take me and what He will accomplish.

While I was writing this book it occurred to me that many of the episodes that I was discussing had humorous interludes. I hope that the humor that I intend to convey in this book will make the reading pleasurable.

Examining my marriages and the mistakes that I have made in the relationships with the women that I have married may be helpful to readers who are examining their own marriages or relationships. I never really had any help in determining how to pick a marriage partner or even how to develop a long-standing relationship. Perhaps my experience can help.

Practicing law for 47 years has taught me a lot. The litigation process and especially courtroom practice is revealing in many and varied ways. Throughout this book I have tried to discuss as many cases as I thought would be of interest to anyone who has wanted to investigate the litigation process. My experience in dealing with fraudulent schemes has had a profound influence on my life and I hope on the lives of those that I was privileged to represent. It seems to me that I was given the opportunity to represent mainly victims and the underrepresented in matters in which business interests took advantage of poor and undereducated individuals that came to me with their problems. I try to give my readers the flavor of not only the cases themselves but also the process by which these cases make their way through court. Some of the cases and descriptions in this book can be considered complicated or complex. The nature of litigation is often complex, and it is my hope that the descriptions that I have given will be of help to people who have themselves been victims and those who want to help the poor and the underrepresented in these currently disruptive times.

When I became a Christian when I was 10 years old, I had no idea where the Spirit would lead me. Both my mother and my father were Christians. My family background led me to a belief in Jesus Christ. When I accepted Christ, I knew that my life had changed and that I would need to more fully understand the workings of the Holy Spirit in my life. It was not until sometime later that I understood that being a Christian put me in the front lines of a spiritual battle that rages all around us all of the time. That spiritual battle many times is very subtle and unless we remain aware, the conflict between good and evil does not appear as a threat to our relationship with God. It is at that exact time that spiritual awareness is most necessary. I hope I have identified how subtly evil can insert itself into our thoughts and behaviors. The Christian that is aware of the spiritual warfare that is going on around us at all times, can and must always seek protection of the Holy Spirit.

The work of the Holy Spirit in my life has caused joy, fullness, peace and understanding. It is my hope that by reading this book that you to will find joy, fullness, peace and understanding. We all seem to grow one step at a time, and it is my intent that the steps that I have taken and described up to this point in my life will be of help to you.

At the time of the writing of this introduction on May 31, 2020, the United States is in the midst of a worldwide pandemic that has claimed the lives of over 100,000 American citizens. Christian sympathy for those who have suffered and for those who minister to the suffering is necessary and commendable. Additionally, the frustration caused by the neglect of the poor and vulnerable portions of our society seems to be erupting throughout the major metropolitan areas of the country. Because we live in a multicultural society there can be mistrust of those who we perceive to be "not like us". It is my belief that we are more alike than different and that if we concentrate on our differences rather than our similarities, we may exacerbate the tensions that occur as a result of mistrust. In the Sermon on the Mount Jesus said "Blessed are the peacemakers, for they will be called the children of God" Matthew 5:9. Today more than ever Christians need to be peacemakers. Also, Jesus admonished us to "do unto others as we would have them do unto us." Matthew 7:21 It is my hope and desire that this book will enable the readers to be mindful of their Christian responsibility and to live the life that Christ intended for each of us.

MARRIAGE

Elaine

The last time I succumbed to marriage was on February 22, 1998. We traveled to St. Thomas, Virgin Island and stayed at an all-inclusive resort. Elaine was tall and had a good figure. Her skin tone was copper. I knew that it was copper because she often asked me to go to Macy's and buy makeup for her that was of that particular skin tone. Like most African Americans, the palms of her hands and the bottoms of her feet were of a lighter color than the rest of her skin. In Elaine's case the palms of her hands and the bottoms of her feet as well as her nipples were red. I later found out that her grandmother on her father's side was a full-blooded American Indian. I often wondered whether that fact caused the unusual coloration of her hands, feet, and nipples. To my way of thinking her skin color and other colorations were very attractive.

I met Elaine in 1986 when she was seeking a divorce from Roger whom she had met while she attended Spellman College. Roger graduated from Morehouse and had gotten a job with a minority owned bank in New York, City. After a few years Roger became a bank executive and he and Elaine would regularly go out with clients and stay out until the bars closed. She finished her degree at Rutgers and worked on her MBA while she held down a job at Chase Bank. When she completed her MBA, she was hired by IBM. Roger enjoyed the benefits of his position as a bank executive and indulged in habits that eventually caused him to serve time (In today's vernacular it is referred to as being sent to school, so

5

you can learn your lesson). Elaine moved back to Atlanta after having lived in Newark for nearly 10 years. Elaine grew up in West Atlanta in an area known as the Collier Heights. At one time that area had been predominantly white. Somewhat close to that area is the historical home of Joel Chandler Harris the author of The Uncle Remus Tales that Walt Disney made into the Song of the South motion picture in the 1950s. During the 50s and 60s West Atlanta changed to predominantly African American. In the early 80s Collier Heights was targeted by a group of black realtors engaging in what became known as foreclosure fraud. Collier Heights is mostly made up of single-family houses with small front lawns. The houses typically have car ports rather than garages. The bedrooms are small, but the houses are livable. The houses in Collier Heights were built to accommodate the families of men returning from World War II. Before I had met Elaine, I had worked on a case against a realty company that had purchased many houses in the Collier Heights neighborhood and therefore I had some familiarity with people who lived in that area of Atlanta.

Elaine is the daughter of Cleveland and Lena. The family attended a Baptist Church until Elaine's father and brother converted to become Jehovah's Witnesses. Elaine's father and brother's conversion split the family. The female members remained Baptist and the male members, because of their beliefs, refused to celebrate holidays, birthdays or recognize any of the celebrations that would normally bring the family together.

Elaine planned our wedding and wanted to get married in Atlanta. She wanted her pastor of the mega-church that she attended to marry us, but he insisted on farming out the wedding to one of the associate ministers in her church. Because of several factors the plan to get married in her church in Atlanta did not materialize and she finally decided that we would fly to St. Thomas, get married and honeymoon at the same time. When she got drunk, and wanted to fight, one of the issues that she often complained about was that I had denied her the wedding of her dreams.

On the day of our wedding, I got up early and went to the beach for a swim in the ocean. An older man from Toronto joined me in the crystal-clear waters. The tide was going out and was strong. The older man started to struggle. It became evident to me that he was not going to make it back to the beach and he was exhausted from his exertion. Fortunately, I was able to help him overcome the tide and drag him to a spot where he could hold on to a rock until the lifeguard was able to throw him a line and pull him to shore. He and his daughter were the only people that attended our wedding. Elaine had no friends, or family, or even witnesses to attend our wedding. While we had pictures taken, there was no celebration or any congratulations from anyone that knew us.

I stayed married to Elaine for eight years but for some reason of which I am only partially aware, I am unable to stay married for more than 12 years at a time. I have wound up going through three divorces. While I have loved each of my wives, we were never able to successfully stay together. I do not fault my former wives for my marriage failures. Even though it is true that it takes two to tango. It only takes one to un-tango. There is no sense in attributing a failed marriage to any one particular reason.

When Elaine and I married I knew that she had a serious drinking problem. We had discussed her drinking and I thought that she was on the road to recovery. She had been laid off by IBM where she had worked for nearly 20 years. I believed that after she found new employment that her excessive drinking would stop, and I continued to date her while she was looking for new employment. After she had been laid off for about six months, IBM realized that they needed her to come back because she had a particular niche that was a large source of revenue for the company. It was then that the evidence showed that the drinking problem was not related to any one particular event, and what was going on in her life that resulted in alcoholism, was probably related to a personality problem that she had endured since she was a child.

Elaine would come home from work, change her clothes, open two bottles of wine, grab a pack of cigarettes, and retreat to the basement. No one at IBM knew that she drank or that she smoked because she did not do that during working hours. Initially, I would sit with her and try to keep up with her drinking. After a while I realized that I could not continue to abuse my body by sitting in the basement and knocking back a few cold ones; so, I started going to bed by myself while she continued to drink and smoke. Usually, she would finish her nightly activities at about 2 or 3 AM. Many times, I would hear her climbing the stairs to our bedroom. Some nights she would awaken me and just want to talk, some nights she wanted to fight. Some nights she wanted sex. Some nights she would cry. I never really knew who was going to come up the stairs after she had finished drinking and smoking. Many times, I would pray when I heard her coming that she would just leave me alone so I could sleep and get up in the morning and go to work. It seemed that the worst of these episodes always occurred when I needed to be in court the next morning.

Elaine insisted that I seek psychological counseling because she knew that the source of her unhappiness was my inability to deal with her problems. By the time she sent me to counseling I was happy to get any help that I could because of the problems that her drinking was causing. Fortunately, the counselor that she chose for me had had experience in dealing with marital problems in which alcohol was a factor. My counselor advised me that I could not stay in a marriage with an alcoholic and advised me to get out of my relationship with Elaine as quickly as I could. It took me about two years to finally decide that I needed to move out. I recall the first time that I left I checked into an extended-stay hotel not far from where we lived. Elaine was always good at using the computer in order to find all kinds of information about our neighbors and people that she knew. She would look up the value of all her friend's houses and all the houses in the neighborhood and she could easily track people down. Within a few days after I had checked into the extended stay hotel Elaine found me. She came to the hotel in the middle of the night. She was drunk. She banged on the door so loudly that she woke everybody up and caused a huge scene. In order to calm her down I agreed that I would return to our home. That same situation was repeated two or three times over the next few months. Elaine always attributed her unhappiness to what I was doing or not doing and never believed that her drinking had any effect on our marriage. She always claimed that wine helped her to relax and did not have any other effect on our relationship. The effects of alcohol on any relationship are very complicated.

9

The movie *Days of Wine and Roses* is an example of what can happen when excessive alcohol use is injected into the marital relationship. In that movie, the initial relationship between the husband and wife was full of roses but after drinking became excessive the marriage began to fall apart and in the end the lives of the characters were destroyed. With that in mind I decided that I had to end my relationship with Elaine and take time to recuperate from all the problems that the excessive use of alcohol had caused.

Trial in Douglas County

One afternoon I was called by a group of deacons from a church in Douglasville, Georgia. Douglasville is outside the perimeter of Atlanta. If you get away from the core of the metropolitan area and get into the suburbs the politics and the culture of the people living in those areas can be radically different from those living inside the perimeter. Douglasville, which is the county seat of Douglas County, is one of those areas in which the conservative flavor of the population is very evident. When I was a young lawyer, I did not like to venture into these outlying counties because there was a lot of home cooking between the judges and the local lawyers. At times I felt it was necessary to engage the services of a local attorney to assist me even in cases in which I felt that the legal issues were very clear.

The deacons from the small church in Douglasville contended that their pastor was competing for the tithes and offerings of the church members by putting offering envelopes in the pews that made payments directly to the pastor, thus bypassing the interests of the church. These deacons asked me to assist them in bringing a lawsuit against the pastor. I have had some experience in the area of church law, and I was also familiar with the duty of loyalty imposed on an employee merely because of his employment. In this situation as often happens, in predominantly black congregations, the pastor of the church is held in high esteem especially by those who do not have higher education. I had attended Elaine's church on a few occasions and was surprised that there were at least three offerings taken up during the service. One offering was for the continuing ministry of the church; one offering was for missionary outreach; and one offering was solely for the support of the pastor. In the church in Douglasville, the pastor had gone beyond the normal collection of tithes and offerings and was actually competing with the church for the regular weekly offerings of the church members.

In that case that I filed in the Superior Court of Douglas County on behalf of the deacons against their pastor, the opposing lawyer was not only an attorney but also a pastor of a small black congregation in Stone Mountain. During the trial, evidence was elicited concerning the pastor's involvement with some of the female members of the church. Because of this, the pastor employed what I deemed to be a bodyguard. The bodyguard maintained a position on the platform next to the pulpit while the pastor conducted the service. When I questioned the pastor concerning his use of a bodyguard, he informed me that the person standing on the platform near the pulpit with him was not actually a bodyguard but was an "armor bearer". I asked the pastor why he needed an armor bearer and he told me that it was biblical.

The case eventually went to the jury and ended in a hung jury. One juror decided that she could not bring herself to find the pastor liable to his congregation. The judge declared a mistrial and about a month later we re-tried the case. At the second trial the jury awarded the exact amount of damages that we had asked for in the first place. By then the pastor the church had resigned, and the deacons felt that they would collect all the money that the pastor had taken. The total amount of the verdict was in excess of $300,000.

In October 2005 I began having problems with my heart. One day when I was at the health club that I belonged to, I passed out after I had stayed on the Stairmaster for a lengthy period of time. I walked into the dressing room passed out, struggled to get up and passed out again. I should have gone to the emergency room then, but Elaine and I had planned a vacation and I thought I would be alright. Elaine and I went on a cruise through the Panama Canal, and I experienced some heart palpitations even while we were still on the cruise. When we came home from our trip, I carried the luggage upstairs and my heart started racing again and I had to lie down until my heartbeat slowed down. A few days later I was walking to my office in Decatur when my heart started racing and I nearly passed out. I had to lean against a telephone pole until I was able to see without cobwebs. I finally made it to my office and the receptionist took one look at me and insisted that I go to the emergency room. I let the receptionist drive me and when I got out of the car and went into the emergency room reception I was immediately put into a wheelchair and taken into a room where I was placed on the drug amiodarone through an intravenous drip. The emergency room doctor came in and examined me and in my usual way I was trying to find the humor in my situation, so I engaged the doctor in light conversation. The doctor said," I would not be talking if I were you because you're about to die." At that moment I realized that there was something very serious going on and that my life was about to change.

I wound up staying in the hospital for 10 days and was diagnosed with ventricular tachycardia a condition that often leads to death. Ventricular tachycardia is usually referred to as a v-tach and occurs when the ventricle of your heart beats rapidly and out of rhythm with the normal process of the pumping action of your heart. Because the ventricle is beating so rapidly blood ceases to be pumped out of your heart and that condition can lead to instant death. While I was in the hospital, for the first time in my life depression came over me and I could not stop crying. I had never had a life-threatening episode and I suppose I realized that I was mortal after all.

On the morning of November 5, 2005, a defibrillator was placed in the left side of my chest. The night before, Elaine told me that she was going home and that she would be back after my surgery. At about 2 AM I heard familiar footsteps coming down the hall of the hospital where I was staying. As usual, she was drunk. Elaine could not figure out how to work the sofa bed in the hospital room, could not figure out how to find sheets, or how to ask the nurse for assistance. Based on her level of sobriety I had no idea how she had actually made it back to the hospital that night. Instead of her being there to comfort me prior to my surgery I had to take care of her.

I finally got back to sleep but it seemed like I was awakened almost immediately and carted off to the ice-cold surgery suite. The doctor that placed the defibrillator in my chest was from the Ivory Coast and I think I was the first patient to have a defibrillator placed by him. I was given several prescriptions known as beta blockers that were designed to regulate my heartbeat. The next day I was sent home but told that I was to come back to the hospital on the following Monday so that they could more exactly calibrate the defibrillator.

I arrived at the hospital at the appointed time and was again taken into the surgery suite. My doctor came in and said in an interesting accent, "You know you have a screw loose". I had to think about that for a few minutes and I finally said, "Some people have told me that before". My doctor insisted that he had to re-open my wound and tighten a screw that he had failed to tighten when he placed the defibrillator a few days before. I was told not to raise my left arm above my waist and to avoid lifting anything for at least six weeks. I was also prohibited from bending at the waist to pick up things on the floor. Despite those restrictions, it was actually good to know that I no longer had a loose screw.

After my hospital stay, I was also prohibited from driving for three months. I walked to the bus stop that was about a half a mile from my house. I had to catch two buses to get to my office. Actually, walking and riding the bus was not too bad. I only saw one fight during the three months that I rode MARTA. The walking was good for me, and I wound up losing a good bit of weight. There was a time or two that I had to wait in the rain but all in all it was not too bad.

When the Christmas holidays arrived after my hospitalization, Elaine and I decided to host my family at our house. My sister and her husband arrived from Meldrim, Georgia, a town that is about 15 miles west of Savannah. My parents drove down from their home in Harnett County, North Carolina. They lived a few miles from Fort Bragg. My father retired from the Navy when I was 13 years old and had military benefits that were available for my parents to use. So, living near Fort Bragg was a benefit to them and also provided my parents with the ability to assist my grandmother who had lived there since she married my grandfather in the early 1920s.

My sister was a government employee, working at the National Oceanographic and Atmospheric Administration's office on Skidaway Island. Her husband was an audio engineer installing sound systems in churches and other locations in and around Savannah. My daughter who was attending college at West Georgia State also came to stay with us for a few days.

The first night after everyone had arrived Elaine became very agitated because I had invited my daughter to come and stay with us. For whatever reason, Elaine did not like my daughter and decided to take her hostility out on me. Everyone had gone to bed and Elaine had gone through her nightly routine. She came upstairs and decided that she wanted to get into a fight. It seemed like an eternity of yelling and screaming. Everyone in the house heard the fighting. There was no place to escape. At one point in the fight Elaine kicked me in my back and knocked the wire that ran from the defibrillator through my vena cava and into my left ventricle, out of its place. Soon the right side of my chest began to pulse as if I was possessed by an alien. The next morning, I had to return to the hospital and wait a few days until the Christmas holidays had ended and the wire could be reinserted into my heart. Needless to say, no one enjoyed that Christmas holiday. It was then that I determined that I could no longer stay married to Elaine and decided that I had to leave that marriage and seek a new direction for my life.

I had never learned how to correctly choose a person with whom I could successfully keep a relationship. As much as I loved my parents and they

16

loved me, they never really helped me make good decisions about dating or gave me any direction concerning how to make a good choice when it came to selecting someone to share my life. I do not believe that my parents ever dated anyone other than themselves. They had no experience in the process of dating or trying to make a decision concerning marriage. When they met, they knew immediately that they loved each other and would to be married. We all need to have life lessons in making proper selections concerning the people that we want to be our closest friends and partners. Maybe because we moved around so much when I was a child, I never made permanent relationships with anyone other than my closest family. The only person that I have known for an extended period of time is my sister, Cathy. For many years even that relationship was tenuous. Cathy is the only person that I have known for more than a few years.

Cathy has always been a cat person and even now she keeps several cats, feeding and petting them every day. When we were children, our cousin gave us a cat. Our mother would not let us keep the cat in the house because she had grown up on a farm and no one kept cats in their house. The cat had to stay in the crawlspace under the house, but the kitten soon died. Later, we received a tomcat. His name was Figaro. I do not remember where the cat came from, but I distinctly remember that Figaro was part of the family when we lived in Jacksonville, Florida. In 1959 we moved from Jacksonville to Quonset Point, Rhode Island, and Figaro made the journey with us. My father had been assigned to the aircraft carrier, Lake Champlain, and the ship had changed ports from Mayport, Florida to Quonset Point, Rhode Island. The Navy moved all of our furniture, but we packed up our 1956 Oldsmobile 88 and mother drove all the way from Florida to Rhode Island. When we crossed the Chesapeake Bay, we took the Kicktapeck Ferry. It was the middle of summer and poor Figaro was miserable. We put a leash on him and took him out on the deck and he panted like a dog.

During that time my father stayed on his ship for long periods of time and our household was run by my mother. Mother grew up on a farm in Harnett County, North Carolina during the Great Depression. My Grandfather on my mother's side had seven children by his first marriage. When his first wife passed away, he married my grandmother and they had seven more children. My mother was the oldest child of my grandfather's second marriage. My mother graduated from high school but at that time, in the county where she lived, high school only went through the 11th grade. During fall harvest, school was let out so that the students could work in the fields to bring in either cotton or tobacco that was grown in the fields surrounding the farm. The Sand Hills region of North Carolina is a very productive farming region. The sandy and loam soil is so fertile that almost anything can be grown there. When World War II started mother left the farm and went to work in a munitions factory in Norfolk, Virginia. One night a group of friends including my mother decided to go out and play miniature golf. My father, by chance, was also playing miniature golf that evening, saw my mother and decided that he was going to marry her at first sight.

The Sakas family is first-generation American. My Grandparents on my father's side immigrated to the United States from Hungary. Actuality their hometown, Sutmar, is now in the Transylvania region of Romania and is known as Sutamarie. That particular area of the world has changed from Hun-

18

gary to Romania and from Romania to Hungary depending on the political climate at the time. When my Grandparents immigrated their country of origin was Hungry. My father only spoke Hungarian until he attended first grade in McKeesport, Pennsylvania. My Grandmother on my father's side died when my father was 12 years old. After my grandmother died, my father and one of my aunts had to go live in Springfield, Illinois for two years, during the depression, because there was no food for all of the siblings. My father was one of six children. My Grandmother was part of the Hungarian aristocracy. Sometimes because of her position (equivalent to a duchess) I tell people that I am the rightful heir to the throne of France.

While still at Duke and still in the Navy, my father was in Norfolk, Virginia because he was on leave from his duties as an officer candidate school student at Duke University. After he graduated from high school, my father enlisted in the Navy. His first duty was as a fireman third class and was assigned to a minesweeper that was stationed at Pearl Harbor on December 7, 1941. According to my father, he had gotten up early and had gone to play softball with other shipmates. When the bombing of Pearl Harbor took place, my father was trying to return to the ship when Japanese fighters strafed the pineapple plantation that he was crossing. My father received a shrapnel wound in his elbow. It was fortunate that he was not on his ship during the attack because his ship was sunk. After the Pearl Harbor attack, my father was transferred to a hospital ship that was assigned to pick up the dead and wounded at the battle of Guadalcanal. My father had no idea that while he was on the hospital ship that his brother, my uncle Andy, had been drafted and was fighting the Japanese on Guadalcanal while my father was on the hospital ship close to that battle.

Shortly after the war started my father was selected to attend officer's candidate school at Duke University and was shipped back to the United States at precisely the right time to be playing miniature golf in Norfolk, Virginia when my mother was also playing miniature golf in Norfolk, Virginia. My parents were married in 1944 and I was born in October 1947. I was born at the Portsmouth Naval Hospital. I tell people that it is very interesting to me that there is a hospital completely dedicated to navels.

The Portsmouth Naval Hospital sits on land that is right at the confluence of the James River and the Chesapeake Bay. That particular physical location has a significant place in American history. It is located within a few miles of Jamestown, Virginia, the first permanent English settlement in America. It is also close to Williamsburg, Virginia the capital of the Virginia colony associated with the American Revolutionary war. Portsmouth is also very close to Yorktown, Virginia where the American Continental army, aided by the French fleet caused the English general, Cornwallis to surrender and effectively end the American Revolutionary war. Portsmouth is also adjacent to the location of the battle between the Merrimack and the Monitor ironclad naval vessels during the American Civil War. Across the water from the hospital is the Norfolk Naval Yard, the largest naval facility in the world.

Our family, during the time that my father was in the Navy, moved from one location to another at least once every three years. Both my sister and I were born in Portsmouth, Virginia. We moved to Camden, New Jersey when I was four. We moved back to Norfolk when I was six. My father was on a ship in the Mediterranean from the time that we moved back to Norfolk until I was in the second grade. The ship was in the Mediterranean because of the 1954 Suez Canal crisis. The Suez Canal crisis came about when Egypt denied Israel the use of the Suez Canal. The United States and other NATO countries decided to guarantee access to the Suez Canal. My father's ship was a troop transport that had a large contingency of Marines that could have been deployed quickly to intervene in any hostility that may have arisen concerning the use of that international waterway.

When I was in the third grade we moved to Hopkinsville, Kentucky. There was a Navy base adjacent to Fort Campbell, Kentucky. Soon after we moved to Kentucky my father was sent to a school in Los Alamos, New Mexico. At the time he was not allowed to tell us what he was studying at the site of the first atomic bomb tests. However, later we determined that my father had to study physics and was working at Clarksville Base to make nuclear weapons.

In the summer between my fourth and fifth grades I attended the Vacation Bible School at the First Baptist Church of Hopkinsville, Kentucky. I felt the call of Jesus Christ on my life and surrendered my life to the service of God. In hindsight, the decision that I made to become a Christian has been the most significant decision of my life.

I had the privilege of seeing both of my parents baptized. When we lived in New Jersey, my mother, who was a devout Christian, decided to be baptized in the church that we attended. Even though I was only four years old, I remember seeing my mother baptized. When my father came back from being in the Mediterranean, he also committed his life to Christ and was baptized at the Norvella Heights Baptist Church in Norfolk.

When I was baptized, I realized that I had made a significant decision. At that time, I was only 11 years old and did not fully understand the calling that had been placed on my life. I realized that I was surrendering myself to the service of Jesus but did not fully understand the significance of my commitment. On the other hand, since the time of my salvation the Spirit of God has never left me, and I have been under the protection of Jesus. I am convinced that God specifically called me to be a member of His family and to share the benefits and obligations of that undertaking for my life. I often wonder how a child of only 10 years old could understand that he was being called into the family of God. I cannot fully answer the question but am convinced that the call was real and that my life was changed. I recall that the hymn "Marching to Zion" was being sung by the congregation when I decided to walk the aisle of the church and declare to the congregation and to God that I would follow Jesus and accept the Holy Spirit into my life. Through the years I have studied the Bible, especially the Gospels and have tried to more fully understand the teachings of Jesus. Most recently, I have taken a course that has explored Jesus' teachings in the Sermon on the Mount (Matthew 5-7 and corresponding versus in the book of Luke). I have also become aware that prominent figures in history, including Leo Tolstoy, Mohandas Gandhi, and Martin Luther King Jr. have relied on Jesus's teachings in the Sermon on the Mount as a basis for their own beliefs, including a belief in non-violence. Perhaps the greatest teaching found in the Sermon is set out in Matthew 7:12 where Jesus states that; "We should do unto others as we would have them do unto us." That admonition of Jesus is basic to his teachings and should be followed by every Christian.

In 1956 people in Hungary revolted against their Soviet controlled government. Prior to World War II Hungarians had experimented with democracy but came under the influence of Nazi Germany during the rise of Hitler. There is obviously a faction of people in Eastern Europe that are subject to authoritarian/right-wing ideology and tend to be anti-Semitic. By 1956 Hungarians influenced by Western liberalism rebelled against Soviet domination. As a result of that rebellion Soviet tanks rolled into Budapest to put down Hungarian attempts to throw off Soviet repression.

Gazah Patkos, who had been trained as a fighter pilot and qualified to fly MIG fighter jets diverted his Russian built airplane from a training mission and crash landed it in West Germany. By the time that the Hungarian revolt was in full swing, Gazah returned to Budapest in order to bring his young wife and newborn child to the West. After he was interrogated by NATO and the CIA, Gazah and his wife Ilona and their young child were sponsored by the First Baptist Church of Hopkinsville, Kentucky and took up residence there. To the best of my knowledge my father was the only person in Hopkinsville at the time that spoke Hungarian and because we were also members of the First Baptist Church, he was recruited to perform translation duties.

The Patkos' family and my family became very close friends. My father taught Gazah and Ilona to speak English. I began to learn a few Hungarian words and my worldview changed dramatically. While my father often spoke Hungarian with his sister and from time to time my father would say a few choice words to me especially when I was doing something that he disapproved. Being around the Patkos family and hearing their stories regarding their escape from Hungary and immigration to the United States gave me a deeper understanding of current history.

When we lived in Hopkinsville, there was a family that lived about four or five houses from us that also had two children, Glenn and Glenda. The son, Glenn, was a year younger than me but I was invited to his birthday party anyway. Glenn's mother bought Glenn a BB gun for his birthday. She set up a target in her backyard and we were all invited to take turns shooting the BB gun at the target. The target was made of plywood. When it was my turn to shoot the BB gun, I could see the BB leave the barrel of the gun and hit the target. I noticed that the BB would bounce off the target and was coming fairly close to where I was shooting the BB gun. I told Glenn's mother that we should move back some more distance because the BBs were ricocheting off the target and were potentially going to hit us. Glenn's mother told me that it was impossible for me to see the BB hit the target and bounce back. I showed Glenn's mother the place where the BB had landed. Again, Glenn's mother told me that I could not possibly see the BB hit the target and bounce back. It was then that I first became acquainted with the concept of "fake news". Some people refuse to be persuaded by reality and choose only to accept their own beliefs. I have experienced this trait in many people over the years. Some of my closest friends do not accept the reality of proven facts. Each of my ex-wives at least on occasions would not accept facts and insisted that whatever understanding they wished to believe was more important than those facts that are proven and usable to lead to making right decisions. The re-

24

fusal to accept facts can often lead to manufactured facts that are also known as lies.

Invariably, when people insist on deviating from provable facts as the basis for making decisions, bad results happen. Not only is this true in individual decision-making or in family decision-making but also in business and even governmental interests. When a leader chooses to base his decisions on anything less than provable facts the risk of failure increases. It would seem to me that the basis for a large amount of wasted effort comes from failure to clearly understand facts. Some people refuse to accept the fact that there is climate change going on in the world. Some people ignore the reality of God. Some people mistakenly believe that they are more important than anyone around them or that we are placed on earth in order to do good and to comfort others. After all, Jesus told his disciples that when the judgment comes, we will be evaluated on the basis of what we have done for others. See Matthew 25: 31-46. If we face judgment based on seeing the needs of others and acting in such a way as to eliminate suffering, then ignoring the needs of others for our own self- interests will ultimately lead to our own destruction.

In the fifth grade I went to school in Jacksonville, Florida. We attended the Southside Baptist Church. After school was out, I again attended Vacation Bible School. The pastor of the church had a son that was my age. As a part of the vacation Bible school program each of the boys my age was to assemble chairs for children that were not old enough to leave the nursery. The chairs that we were to assemble came in a kit. It was our job to put the pieces of the chairs together, sand the chairs so that they would be smooth, varnish the chairs and paint the chairs. The leaders of the Vacation Bible School were to decide who had assembled the chair in the most satisfactory manner and award a prize to the student that produced the best chair. When I was putting my chair together, I realized that the edge of the chair where a child's legs would come in contact with the wood had a sharp edge. As part of my assembly, I sanded off the sharp edge so as to make the chair more comfortable for the younger child that would sit on it. When the Bible School leaders inspected the chairs the prize for the best chair was awarded to the pastor's son. I asked the leader why my chair was not selected, and he said that someone had sanded off the sharp edge and that the decision was made that my chair was not good enough. It was then that I learned that it's not whether you do a good job at the task that you are given, but that your position, or family, or reputation counted more than any improvements that you may think will help others. This also seems to be a persistent occurrence even in the practice of law. There have been many occasions when I have presented the best argument to a judge only to be told that my opponent would have the victory. When I looked more closely into the relationship between the judge and my opponent, I determined that there had been a close relationship between the judge and the other lawyer in the past. Also, on occasions I have made arguments before a judge that I felt were inadequate but received a favorable judgment just because the judge knew me. While justice should be blind, that evidently is not the case in many instances.

In October of 1957, the Soviet Union launched the first earth orbiting satellite, Sputnik, and I became aware of how the "Cold War" was affecting not only the United States but also my family. President Eisenhower came on TV and talked about how the

United States was falling behind in the exploration of space and rocket development. There were failures by the American military to launch satellites from Cape Canaveral. The Russians were able to put a dog into orbit and later the cosmonaut Yuri Gagarin. In an effort to catch up with the Russians, American astronauts were chosen. The first American astronaut to be sent into space was Alan Sheppard. Sheppard was launched from Cape Canaveral and the space capsule came down in the South Atlantic. The aircraft carrier that my father was on, the Lake Champlain was designated as the recovery vessel for that first American spaceflight. As part of my father's duties on the ship, he was in communication with Cape Canaveral and the recovery helicopters that were dispatched to pick up Sheppard and the space capsule. A day or two after the Sheppard suborbital mission had taken place my mother received a letter from my father describing in detail his observation of the landing of the space capsule carrying Alan Sheppard. My father's time in the Navy started with his ship being sunk at Pearl Harbor and ended with the recovery of the first American space adventure.

During the summer of 1958 we moved to Rhode Island. While we lived in Rhode Island my family and I attended the Gwinnesset Baptist Church in East Greenwich, Rhode Island. That church had been founded in about 1670. The graveyard associated with the church had gravestones as far back as the late 1600s. Gwinnesset Baptist was an independent congregation with no connection to any other Baptist assemblies or conventions. The pastor of the church, Ed Steady was from Buffalo, New York. He preached the gospel but admonished the congregation not to vote for John Kennedy for president because Pastor Steady was afraid that Kennedy would take his direction from the Pope. My parents were Republicans and voted for Nixon in the 1960 election. When Kennedy was elected there was a feeling of despair in our household.

When my father retired from the Navy in 1961, we moved to Clarksville, Tennessee. We moved into the married students housing at Austin Peay State College. Even though my father had attended Duke he had not received his bachelor's degree because when he decided to marry my mother, he was forced to resign from the OCS program at Duke and was required to return to the ranks as an enlisted man. My father worked his way up the ranks and became a Chief Warrant Officer by the time he retired.

My father planned to obtain a teaching certificate and teach high school math after he left the Navy. When he was able to finish his bachelor's degree in short order, he was persuaded to continue his education and to get a master's degree in guidance and counseling. Because he had benefits remaining on the G.I. Bill, he decided that he would pursue his doctorate degree and in 1963 we moved from Clarksville to Nashville. I started high school at West End High School and decided to play football. My father was pursuing his doctorate degree at Peabody College (Peabody College later became a part of Vanderbilt and my father's degree was changed to reflect that he was a graduate of Vanderbilt University).

Because my father was pursuing his degree and was a full-time student, we had to scrape by financially with my father's retirement check from the Navy and whatever benefits he was able to obtain through the G.I. Bill. Mother from time to time would seek temporary employment to help supplement the family's income. As a result of our financial situation, I was not able to engage in many social activities at school, but I did play football, basketball and baseball. We attended the First Baptist Church of Nashville; Tennessee and the church had many activities for someone like me. We went to church every Sunday, attended Sunday evening services, and regularly attended Wednesday night prayer meeting. After prayer meeting the youth choir practiced and I sang in the choir which was the choir that filled the choir loft at the early service on Sunday mornings. First Baptist Church was located in downtown Nashville. We lived near Vanderbilt but would usually ride to church in an area that was full of recording studios, also known as Music Row. I recall on one Sunday morning when we were riding to church that I looked over and the Beatles were in the adjacent car.

My father received his doctorate degree and I graduated from high school in the spring of 1966. I started college that summer and realized that for some unknown reason I was attractive to older girls. When I started college, the anti-war movement was starting to receive a great deal of media coverage. I think it is clear that there was a cultural revolution going on in the United States during the late 1960s. The causes of the "Cultural Revolution" that took place in the 1960s have been debated by many scholars. I think there was a divergence of causes with the civil rights movement and the anti-war movement being only a part of the catalysts. It was a time in which baby boomers were coming-of-age. Birth control pills had been developed and engendered a sexual freedom that was unknown up to that point in the United States. At that time the AIDS epidemic that did not start until the 1980s did not impose a risk for sexual activity. There seemed to be an openness to start a different lifestyle than that projected by television sitcoms of the late 50s and early 60s in such television shows as *"Father Knows Best"*, *"Ozzie and Harriet"*, *"Leave It to Beaver"* and others. There was also a desire for complete freedom of expression that could be heard in rock 'n roll music. But it was the civil rights movement and the anti-war movement that acted as the main catalysts of profound changes in the American culture.

At first, because of my parent's influence, I believed that the Vietnam War was in America's national interests. After all we were seeking to stop the spread of communism, or so it seemed. I was asked to write a column in the high school newspaper called "From the Right". My friend, Lloyd Parker, wrote the "From the Left" column. Gradually I began to see that the war in Vietnam would be impossible to win and that it was not in our national interest to pursue that war at the expense of so many young lives. Fortunately, after I registered for the draft, I had a student deferment and then after the student deferment exemption was revoked, I received a fairly high draft number in the draft lottery that took place while I was in college. It did not hurt that my draft board was in downtown Nashville and their quota was for the most part filled by volunteers. They do not call Tennessee the "Volunteer State" for nothing. There were two different types of people from my high school that went to Vietnam. Floyd, who was a year ahead of me in school, volunteered for the Army. After spending one tour of duty in Vietnam he came back to the high school and bragged about blasting everything in sight with his M-16. On the other hand Ray, whose locker was next to mine in the football locker room, enrolled at the University of Tennessee right after high school, flunked out, got drafted, and now his name appears on the Vietnam Memorial. I do not know what happened to Floyd but if he is still alive, I think he may lean to the right and would more likely than not to refuse to be vaccinated against COVID.

When I went to college at Middle Tennessee State University (MTSU), ROTC was required for all male freshmen and sophomore students. The first time I had to put on my army uniform it was a very traumatic thing for me. As I mentioned while I was still in high school, I became convinced that the war in Vietnam was an American tragedy. One day I was walking across campus and going into a classroom building. My army cap was securely in my hand as I walked across the campus. Just as I was entering the Old Main classroom building the colonel in charge of the ROTC program was exiting and saluted me. I had never been saluted before and had never saluted anyone. I threw up my left hand and gave him a salute that was unacceptable. The colonel took exception to my halfhearted attempt at a left-handed salute and chewed me out right there in the doorway of the classroom building. He also wanted to know why I was not wearing my hat, to which I replied I didn't like it, it wasn't my style, and I was in the ROTC under protest. The colonel did not accept my explanation.

All the ROTC underclassmen were required to have their uniforms on (including their hats) and attend a drill once a week. At these drills upperclassman who had decided to seek a career in the Army were allowed to order the underclassmen around and get in their face. I saw my opportunity. At the next drill I altered my uniform, I found an old-World War I German helmet with a spike on top, a pair of red socks, and a CSA (Confederate States of America) belt buckle (after all the mascot for Middle Tennessee was a Confederate soldier also known as the

Blue Raider. The Blue Raider was Nathan Bedford Forrest, a famous Calvary general from Pulaski, Tennessee.) I put a daisy in the barrel of the M1 rifle that I was required to carry. The upperclassman that was in charge of the group of ROTC students that I was part of, did not think my uniform alteration was very funny and told me that I had to leave the drill. I had to take ROTC during the summer semester in order to graduate from college.

I played baseball while I attended Middle Tennessee. I hit .300 my senior year and would have played on if any professional team would have shown any interest. The baseball caps that we wore had the letters MT on them. I often wondered if those who designed the hats realized that the symbol of MT could also be pronounced as empty. There were several of the players on our team to which the term empty applied. One of the catchers on our team was offered a bonus of fifteen hundred dollars to sign a professional contract right out of high school. He told the team that was recruiting him that he was holding out for thousand dollars.

Phyllis

My time at Middle was enjoyable. I was always on the Dean's list and felt as if I greatly benefited from the courses that I took. I had a dual major. I took all the education courses necessary in order to qualify for a teacher's certificate when I graduated. But what I really liked most were the courses in political science that I took. The chairman of the political science department was Norman Parks. Doctor Parks before coming to Middle Tennessee had also been a professor at Vanderbilt and also had been on the editorial board of the Nashville Tennessean. Doctor Parks was also a close friend of Albert Gore, the senator from Tennessee that is the father of Albert Gore who became Vice President of the United States. Doctor Parks also had a relationship with the Dean of the law school at Tulane University in New Orleans. Based on Doctor Parks recommendation Tulane would accept a student from MTSU, no questions asked. During my senior year in college, I applied to several law schools and was accepted at Tulane Law School and my first wife, and I moved to New Orleans in August 1970.

I met Phyllis between my sophomore and junior year in high school. She went to a high school on the other side of Nashville from where my family lived. Her family was from just west of Buffalo, New York. We both attended the First Baptist Church of Nashville and we both sang in the youth choir. In the summer of 1964, the youth choir went on a choir tour from Nashville to the Six Flags amusement park between Dallas and Fort Worth, Texas. We performed concerts along the way in churches in Alabama, Mississippi and Texas. Generally, we performed a concert in an evening service and church members from that particular church would put us up for the evening. While we were traveling Phyllis and I became friends and by the time we arrived at Six Flags over Texas we were a couple. In her family, Phyllis was the second oldest of four girls and one boy. Each of Phyllis's sisters had become cheerleaders at their high school. During my junior year Phyllis and I broke up and my heart was broken. One night during my junior year in college I drove up to Nashville to see some friends. By chance I bumped into Phyllis who was attending Belmont College and we started dating again.

Between my junior and senior year in college I got a job at Eastman Kodak Company in Rochester, New York. During that summer Phyllis and her family had gone to live with Phyllis's Grandparents in Derby, New York. She invited me to come to spend the weekend with her family and I took the bus from Rochester to Buffalo. Phyllis met me at the Buffalo Greyhound station, and we decided to drive over to Niagara Falls that evening. Phyllis had borrowed her cousins Corvair automobile and off we went.

That Corvair was probably getting more miles to the gallon of gas than to the quart of oil, and it was polluting anyone who came close to us. We finally crossed over the Peace Bridge and entered into the Canadian side of the falls. We parked the car on the street which was allowed at that time and took a stroll by the falls. After a time of handholding, we went to get the car to go back to her cousin's house. The car was gone. Phyllis was 18 and I was 19. We panicked. We decided we would try to find a Monty (Canadian mounted police) and report the stolen car. As we were walking down the street, we found the car parked in the middle of the street. Evidently, whoever had taken the car decided that it was so bad that they just abandoned it in the middle of the street. The book *Unsafe at Any Speed* didn't come out until a few years later but those who took the car must have realized that the danger of riding in that Corvair after having stolen it, was greater than the reward of having that piece of junk.

Later that summer Phyllis and I became engaged. Both of us were too young to know what we were doing. It was fashionable in the late 60s for people in their early 20s to get married. Neither one of us had enough life experience, financial capabilities, or spiritual guidance to make our marriage work. As I mentioned earlier, I did not receive help from my parents or anyone else for that matter, to help me understand either how to select a wife or even to make a good friendship. I don't think that either Phyllis or I understood what a commitment really meant. We did not have enough common experiences on which we could rely to hold us together. Neither of us understood that in the summer of 1968 and we certainly did not understand that going forward.

The spring and summer of 1968 were particularly dramatic in the history of the United States. In late spring Martin Luther King Jr. was assassinated in Memphis, Tennessee. That evening I had a date with Phyllis and had driven around Nashville in order to avoid riots that were going on especially around Tennessee State University. After our date, I decided to drive back through the area where the riots were going on and witnessed gunfire between National Guard troops and students that were barricaded in their dormitories at Tennessee State. Later that summer, while I was living in Rochester, NY Robert Kennedy the younger brother of President John Kennedy was assassinated in California where he had been campaigning for the presidency. Later that summer, during the Democratic national convention in Chicago, race riots erupted throughout the United States.

That fall both Phyllis and I went back to college. We continued to see each other and set a date for our wedding for August 16, 1969. That next spring Middle had a baseball game in Nashville and Phyllis showed up at the game. She must have noticed that I was chewing tobacco because she came up behind me and slapped me on the back in order to see if I would swallow my chaw. I didn't and she learned for the first time that I was capable of doing things that did not please her. As our relationship progressed, we both came to understand that neither one of us was capable of totally disregarding the others feelings. Shortly after the first man landed on the lunar surface on June 20, 1969, we were well into the wedding rituals. By the time that August rolled around I realized that it was a mistake for me to marry Phyllis. I prayed that God would cause me to fall in love with Phyllis or that fate would cause the wedding to be cancelled. That prayer was not answered affirmatively. In retrospect I should have prayed for the courage to tell Phyllis that it was a mistake for us to be married. Our lives would have been very different. On the other hand, we do have two children who both of us love and who give us a great deal of satisfaction.

After our wedding we drove to New Orleans for our honeymoon. As we approached New Orleans hurricane Camille was about to hit the Gulf Coast. By the time we reached Slidell, Louisiana the outer bands of the hurricane could be felt. We had to make a decision of whether to stay in Slidell or continue on to New Orleans. We were driving a Volkswagen beetle and the winds were really blowing that car around on the road. We decided that we would try to make it to New Orleans. As we crossed the I-10 bridge over Lake Ponchatrain, the waves were coming over the bridge. Needless to say, Phyllis was very frightened and even though I was somewhat afraid, I had to put on a strong front to get us into New Orleans. Had we stayed in Slidell we may have been killed. New Orleans was spared. But the entire Gulf Coast from Pass Christian, Mississippi to Panama City, Florida was devastated. Phyllis had an aunt and cousins who lived in Biloxi, Mississippi. We were going to try to visit them on her way home, but Camille had so devastated that area so much that no one was allowed to travel along the Gulf Coast.

Phyllis and I settled into our apartment at the married student's apartments at Middle Tennessee. I generally hung out with the guys on the baseball team until early evening. One afternoon while I was working out with the baseball team Phyllis got an obscene call. It turned out that one of the younger men in the married student complex had seen Phyllis and started making lewd and obscene calls. We generally had a very nice time that last year in college, but we became aware that sexual predators and perverts can be found in just about any location. After that summer Phyllis continued to take courses at Middle Tennessee while I found work in Nashville.

I graduated from Middle in May 1970. That summer I worked at various jobs and was able to save enough money to help us meet our expenses after I enrolled at Tulane Law School the following September. Towards the end of the summer my sister announced that she had married a man named Richard. She had taken a summer job as a lifeguard at Fort Stewart Army base in Hinesville, Georgia. Evidently, she didn't like to stay in Hinesville very long and found a job in Savannah. She met Richard and they started living together. In 1970 Georgia still recognized common-law marriage. Cathy called home and asked that my parents bring her clothes and her birth certificate to Savannah so that they could also meet their new son-in-law, Richard. My parents asked me and Phyllis to go with them. My mother who was going through menopause at the time, cried all the way from Murfreesboro to Savannah.

We arrived in Savannah in the late afternoon. We found Cathy's apartment on Abercorn Street and found Cathy and Richard in their second-floor apartment. Cathy had cats. Richard had shoulder length hair and bell bottom pants. There were roaches of both kinds in the apartment. The place smelled of incense and stale smoke. Richard was working as a freelance photographer selling photographs to the local newspapers. Cathy had a job as a long-distance operator at the phone company. Cathy also was taking classes at Armstrong State College and was interested in pursuing a degree in marine biology. Savannah is a beautiful old southern town that was spared by General Sherman in his march to the sea during the Civil War. Savannah was a planned city. It is on the Savannah River and has been a port city since it was founded. The downtown area was laid out with a series of parks at regular intervals. Cathy has always been proud of her adopted home and has remained a resident of Savannah for all the rest of her life.

Over the years I have visited Savannah on a somewhat regular basis. Eventually, Cathy bought a cottage on Tybee Island which is also known as Savannah Beach. She calls her cottage Octopus Lair and has it decorated in that motif. I have taken my children to the beach there and there have been many holidays celebrated either at the beach or at some other house that Cathy has shared with husbands and boyfriends. One of the last holidays that we shared with my grandmother was on Tybee Island. Cathy and her second husband John Crawford (also known as "Crawfish") had rented a house on Tybee and invited the whole family to come and spend Christmas with her. At the time I was married to Iliana, and we brought my children to this gala event. My parents along with my grandmother drove down from North Carolina. Needless to say, there was a house full of people.

Cathy's husband, Crawfish, (his real name is John Crawford, but almost everyone calls him "Crawfish") had a collection of snakes that he kept in containers in the master bedroom. Our first night of the Christmas vacation started in an auspicious manner. Crawfish announced that he was missing a copperhead snake from his collection and that we should be on the lookout for it. That night because of the crowd of people I had to sleep in the sleeping bag on the floor and was very wary of meeting Crawfish's snake. The next morning, Grandma said that somebody had left a belt under the sofa that she was sitting on. It was not a belt; it was the copperhead that had gotten loose. Fortunately, because it was somewhat cool the snake was not active, and Crawfish was able to restore it to its cage. We were able to celebrate Merry Christmas nonetheless

Law School

Within a few days after we returned to Tennessee from being with Cathy and Richard on our first trip to Savannah, it was time for Phyllis and me to move to New Orleans and for me to enroll in law school at Tulane. When we moved to New Orleans, we did not have any furniture and only had a few clothes. Phyllis did have a rather large supply of shoes but that is another story. Upon arriving in New Orleans, we searched for an apartment, and we were lucky to find an efficiency apartment in a shotgun house on Broad Street that is fairly close to Tulane's campus. Luckily, the apartment was furnished we did not have to buy any furniture. Phyllis found a job at the Tulane athletic department, selling tickets to the football games. The apartment that we had was within walking distance of her job and the law school. We did not have a car. We did not know anybody and were totally on our own in a new place that was different from anything that either of us had ever known.

After we had been in New Orleans a few days we decided to go out one evening to the movies. We walked down to the streetcar line and traveled from the Garden District of New Orleans to Canal Street. There was a theater there showing the newly released movie *Catch 22*. They sold mixed drinks at the theater, something that I had never seen before. Of course, there was much in New Orleans that I had never seen before. After the movie was over, we decided to ride the streetcar back to where we had started from. We waited along the streetcar line but for some reason after a long wait no streetcar came. Finally, a bus came to the bus stop, and it had a Ferret Street sign on it. The law school was also on Ferret Street.

I decided that we could take the bus and it would at least take us close to the law school that was in walking distance from our apartment. Two days before there had been a race riot in New Orleans. That riot ended in a shoot-out In the Desire Street Housing Project. When we got on the Ferret Street bus, I had no idea about the route the bus would take to get back to the Tulane campus. When we got on the bus, we were the only ones on it. Soon the bus drove through the Desire housing project and because it was Saturday night the bus became filled with black people who evidently had been having a good time. As the bus became more and more crowded Phyllis and I were the only white people in a bus filled with blacks even the bus driver was black. Neither of us had ever experienced a situation in which we felt so uncomfortable because we were so unlike all the rest of the people around us. The bus took us through several housing projects and before long the bus was full. The bus finally got near the Tulane campus, and I decided that we needed to get out of the bus and make our way to our apartment. Just as the bus door opened a flood of people pushed to get on the bus. By that time, it was probably around midnight. It just so happened that the Saints were playing an exhibition football game that night at the Tulane Stadium. The game had just ended when we arrived at the place where I decided to get off the bus. Both of us were frightened and we ran the five or six blocks from where we got off the bus to our apartment. We did not bother to turn on the lights, did not bother to get out of our clothes, we just jumped in to bed and pulled the covers over our heads.

A few days later there was an orientation for first-year law students at the law school. The law school had just moved into a new building and there was a patio on which the school was serving hot dogs and hamburgers and lots of beer. At the orientation, the Dean of the law school who was from Switzerland told the incoming students that we needed to learn how to control our drinking and that "the law is a jealous mistress" and that often times the study and practice of law comes between lawyers and their significant others. At Tulane the first-year students were required to take the same basic courses. The freshman class met in a classroom on the first floor of the law school, and we met in the same room for each lecture session. Different law professors came into that room to lecture us on torts, contracts, criminal law, and civil procedure.

The civil procedure Professor, Leon Hubert, had been the District Attorney of Orleans Parish just before Jim Garrison who prosecuted Jack Ruby as a conspirator in the assassination of President Kennedy. Professor Hubert evidently was a Phi Beta Kappa scholar. He usually dressed in a three-piece black suit and continually stroked what appeared to be a Phi Beta Kappa key coming out of his watch pocket. He had a thin pencil mustache, and his hair was jet black and slicked down straight back on his head. He spoke in a very deep Southern drawl. Professor Hubert was instrumental in drafting the Louisiana Civil Procedure Code that was more or less based on the Federal Rules of Civil Procedure.

The first day that Professor Hubert lectured regarding civil procedure, he asked this question, "What is the purpose of civil procedure?" Because it was the first day of class no one answered and after a few minutes went by without a sound, the professor then went to the chalkboard and drew a large $. He turned to the class and said, "the purpose of civil procedure is dollars; it is how you convert a cause of action into money." I often think of that first lecture and Professor Hubert's viewpoint of the purpose of civil procedure. It was very enlightening. Law is an avenue by which people have determined a system that allows a result to be fashioned from oftentimes random occurrences. Law is ultimately a system by which society can achieve results on a more or less predictable basis. I have tried to keep that perspective in the 46 years that I have been actively practicing law. Many times, we tend to lose the perspective of law being a system that should result in predictable results. Unfortunately, many lawyers think that the law is a free-for-all competition in which one can practice one-up-man-ship and can change results on an unpredictable basis.

While we did not have assigned seats in the classroom, I wound up sitting next to a man that was missing a leg and some fingers and had scars all over his body. In our contracts course we were required to read cases and be prepared to orally discuss the cases that had been assigned for briefing the day before in class if called upon by the professor. Contracts was taught by Professor Hoffman Fuller. One day Professor Fuller called on Mr. Berthalo, the man who was sitting next to me to recite. Hank Berthalo got up and started to talk in a very raspy voice. Professor Fuller asked him to speak up and Hank replied in his raspy voice "Sir, cannot speak up, vocal cords shot out, sir".

Later that morning I asked Hank what had happened to him, and he related the following story: "When I got out of high school, I wanted to join the Army. I always wanted to be a soldier. I signed up and after basic training I was sent to Vietnam." I asked were you were injured in Vietnam? He said, "let me finish my story". Hank went on "After I had served a tour in Vietnam the Army liked me and I liked the Army. I was sent to West Point, and I played football for Army. After I graduated, I was again sent to Vietnam. I was promoted to Captain and was in charge of a company of men that were sent to the Iron Triangle (a part of the country that was highly contested by the Viet Cong) during the war in Vietnam. We got into a firefight and my position was overrun by Viet Cong. I called for a rocket attack on my own position. I was the only survivor and was severely wounded. I was later given the Congressional Medal of Honor for my service." I was sitting next to a war hero. When I first saw Hank, I was somewhat taken aback by his injuries. When I heard his story, I was proud to have sat beside such a man. Hank was married and had two small boys. He told me that he wanted to stay in the Army, but they would not let him because of his disabilities. In my mind it was a waste. If the Army could not have found a place for him, then it was the Army's loss.

Perhaps the same is true in other areas of our lives. We have a plan, we decide to make the most of our opportunities, and start down a path that looks like the right direction. Sometimes we can go down that path for many years and at the end we find fulfillment in our lives. Many times, however, while we believe we are going in the right direction there is an intervention. I think in my life that God has intervened on several occasions to change the direction and velocity of the path that I was taking. In Hank's case calling a rocket strike down on his own position, while being the right thing to do at the time, took him from being a soldier to being an attorney. I thought my life would be one continuous path, directed by God, to a certain conclusion. I have found, however, that the outcome may not be for us to know, but it is always important to believe that God's hand is leading us.

After my first year in law school, I was looking for a summer job. Phyllis and I had been attending regular meetings at the Baptist Student Union. I had been praying that I would find a summer job. Out of the blue I got a call from the director of the BSU asking if I would be interested in a position as a summer missionary in Washington DC. I believed this opportunity was an answer to my prayers. Within a few days Phyllis and I were able to get on an airplane and fly from New Orleans to Washington. We were greeted at the airport, and I was told that my job would require me to work in the office of Senator Edmund Muskie of Maine. On the weekends I had other duties including driving the VW van that belonged to the Southern Baptist Home Mission Board, down to the prison in Lorton, Va. to pick up prisoners, bring them back to the Johenning Baptist Center in Anacostia so that they could act as tutors to the children who had reading disabilities.

The Johenning Baptist Center was located in the southeast corner of the District of Columbia. At that time in 1971 that area of DC is mainly government housing projects and was 100% black. Many of the children that came to the center had never seen a white person. I usually wore shorts and T-shirts, and the children were amazed to see the hair on my arms and legs. Many times, I would look down and one of the children was just rubbing away on my leg or arm. Invariably the child would look up at me and say, "how you get so furry". I learned to love those children. God had certainly put me in a place that I needed to be. When I signed up to be a summer missionary, I did not know what was to be expected, I only had to believe.

On Capitol Hill one of my duties was to respond to letters from Senator Muskie's constituents. Another of my duties was to call a certain number on the telephone that was linked to the Democratic caucus. A recording would come on and provide information concerning committee meetings and votes that were going to occur during the day. I would usually prepare a short memorandum outlining those matters and give it to a more permanent staff member. On a few occasions I was asked to draft a speech for the senator to make.

During that time Senator Muskie had announced that he was running for president, and he assembled a brain trust of the leading liberal economists in order to help him set his economic policy. A meeting of these noted economists was set, and the location of the meeting was in the sub- subterranean office that Muskie had under the United States Capitol building. It was my job to assist some of the economists in locating the place of the meeting and attend to their needs. Some of the notable attendants were Paul Samuelson, the author of the most widely used college textbook on economics, Arthur Okun, and Charles Schultz (who later became President Jimmy Carter's chief economic advisor).

One of the main topics being discussed at the time of the meeting of these economists was what to do about the financial difficulties of Lockheed Corporation, the manufacturer of airplanes. I was very impressed with Charles Schultz who had a plan for the United States to lend money to Lockheed at interest in order to bail them out of their economic problems. He outlined the program as if he were outlining a prepared text. Eventually, Congress adopted Charles Schultz recommendation and Lockheed was bailed out. The United States made money on the deal. Years later the same formula that Schultz had outlined regarding the Lockheed bailout was used by the government to bail out the auto industry during the 2008 recession.

Later that summer, I called Jim Stovall one of my friends, with whom I studied at Tulane, to find out my scores on my final exams. Jim was excited to tell me that I had done very well. I had one of the best grades in Constitutional Law and had good scores in my other classes as well. After my first year of law school I was in the top 10% of my class. My class consisted of 190 students of which 80% were male. The top 10% of the class at Tulane were put on the Law Review and the second 10% were put on the Moot Court. I was number 19 and the Law Review only took 18 that year. So, I became a judge of the moot court. I had to write a problem for the first-year students to research and then the first-year students would make an oral presentation either in defense of or in opposition to the premises of the problem that I had written. One of the issues that I had researched when I was working in Washington, the previous summer, concerned how to require corporations to consider shareholder inputs into corporate decision-making. That became the basis for the legal problem that I wrote for the first-year students. As part of that assignment, I also had to grade those student's research papers and act as a judge of their oral argument.

As a part of the tradition at Tulane the members of the Moot Court and the Law Review played a touch football game every fall. The loser of the game from the year before had to challenge the other honors group the following year to the football game. An elaborate challenge was written. In the challenge usually written in humorous, if not slanderous tones, one team charged the other one with being "jockus incompetence" and of having "foul balls". The game was played on the quadrangle in front of the student union building. Because I had played baseball and college, I was asked to be the quarterback of the moot court team. It was a close game and it ended when I threw a touchdown pass to Carl Trischman, and we won.

When we lived in New Orleans Phyllis, and I joined the St. Charles Avenue Baptist Church. The pastor of the church was Avery Lee. His wife, Anne, had bandages on her face and around her head; she drooled excessively and could not talk clearly. I was appalled by her appearance. Anne Lee had contracted cancer and it settled into the bones of her face. That form of cancer is exceedingly painful, but Anne never complained, she was always helpful to those in need of her help. She died gracefully, embodying a Christian spirit that has remained as a model for me. Even now I think back on her struggles, the pain that she was in, but more importantly the grace that she exhibited while going through those stages of cancer.

Newt Gingrich also attended the St. Charles Avenue Baptist Church when he was a student at Tulane. Newt made a profession of faith while he was attending St. Charles Avenue and was baptized. As you may know Baptists believe in complete immersion in water as a symbol of a changed life. Many years later I saw Pastor Lee while visiting New Orleans and we discussed Newt Gingrich. By then Newt had become a congressman from Georgia and eventually ascended to become Speaker of the House of Representatives. We also discussed Newt Gingrich's conversion and his baptism. Pastor Lee commented that he thought that Newt's conversion to Christianity was not complete. I suggested that the pastor should have held him under longer in the baptism pool. Dr. Lee commented that had he held him down for about 10 minutes many things would have been different in the United States.

Moving to Atlanta

After my sophomore year in law school, I was able to get a summer clerkship at a large law firm in New Orleans. At the end of the summer, I was offered a job when I graduated at that law firm. Phyllis had been ill most of the year and did not want to stay in New Orleans. It was my firm belief that one day New Orleans was going to sink, and it was better for me to find a job in some other city. New Orleans is a very unique place. If you have never visited New Orleans, you should. Advancement in New Orleans required that you be a member of those favored by that society. While I could have worked at the major law firm, I believed that because of the closed nature of New Orleans that I would not have advanced to partnership in that firm. I looked for other opportunities and after graduating decided to move to Atlanta.

Phyllis and I moved to Atlanta in the summer of 1973. I had found a job at a small law firm in downtown. When I went to work, I thought I was going to be a tax and estate lawyer and not deal with litigation. The first day I came to the office the senior partner told me that I needed to go to court to assist Fred Cavalli who was trying a case against the City of Atlanta. Fred had sued the City of Atlanta on the theory of nuisance, meaning that the city had damaged the property of Fred's client in the manner in which the city used its property. In that case the city had allowed the accumulation of debris in the storm drain close to our client's house. Because of the debris in the storm sewer, water was diverted and came in contact with the foundation of our client's house. After some time, the foundation of our client's house washed away, and our client's house collapsed. The city had refused to make repairs or to remove the debris from the storm sewer. The cities key witness was Eldrin Bell, a young police officer who later became chief of police. It was rumored that Eldrin Bell, who was a black man with blue eyes, was Mayor Manard Jackson's half-brother. It was rumored that both Mayor Jackson and Eldrin Bell had the same father. The jury returned a verdict in favor of our client. As soon as that case was over, we started into another case in front of the same judge. For the first couple of weeks of my law career I stayed in court assisting in two trials.

For about two months during the summer of 1973, I studied for the bar exam. I took the bar exam and sweated out the results. On a Monday evening in November of that year I received a call from one of the partners in the law firm for which I was working. He said that the bar results were out and that if I called the newspaper I could find out if I had passed. I could not get through to the newspaper that evening and tossed and turned all night. The next morning, I decided to call the clerk's office of the Superior Court of DeKalb County. I asked the clerk if she had the bar results and she said that she did. I asked her to start reading the names of those who had passed the bar exam starting with last names beginning with the letter S. She read four or five names and then she read my name. I told her that she could stop reading because I was relieved. Within a few days I was sworn in.

I had been working on a case involving a pre-judgment garnishment. Pre-judgment garnishment means that my client was trying to garnish a creditor's bank account prior to obtaining a judgment for the amount owed. At that time Georgia law allowed pre-judgment garnishment if the garnisher posted a bond. In that case the opposing lawyer filed a constitutional objection to the proceeding in the State Court of Clayton County claiming that the Georgia pre-judgment garnishment statute was unconstitutional because it amounted to an unlawful taking of property in violation of the fourth amendment to the United States Constitution. The case went before a three-judge panel in the United States District Court in Atlanta. That case was eventually consolidated with another case and went to the United States Supreme Court for decision. The Supreme Court determined that the Georgia pre-judgment garnishment law was in fact unconstitutional.

The lawyer that I worked most closely with was a man by the name of Israel Katz. Mr. Katz had other business interests that kept him out of the full-time law practice. He finally decided that his outside business interests were more important to him than the law practice and told me that I should try to find other work. George Duncan and I had played baseball together in Nashville when we were both in high school. Both of us attended the First Baptist Church of Nashville and had become good friends. George went to Emory and then on to Emory Law school in Atlanta. Out of law school George had joined the firm of Shoob, McLean & Jesse whose offices were in the First National Bank building just down the street from the office in which I was working.

One day when I was going to lunch, I happened to bump into George on Peachtree Street, and he suggested that there was an opportunity to work with a new firm that was being formed in which he was involved. Later that summer I went to work for the newly established firm of Jesse, Richie & Duncan. Jim Jesse was the senior partner and was 20 years older than any of the other partners. Again it was my understanding that I was being hired to deal with non-litigation matters including business formations and tax advice. It turned out that most of the advice that I was giving was to Jim Jesse, and most of the advice dealt with how he could utilize the law practice to pay his own personal expenses with pre-tax dollars. Later, Jesse's use of the law business became abusive and became the basis for the breakup of that firm.

The Birth of Nicholas

A profoundly life-changing experience in my life occurred in September 1976. Phyllis had become pregnant earlier that year. She was due to give birth during the first week of October. On the morning of September 25, I met up with a friend of mine to chop wood that we could use in our fireplace. I worked very hard all day and was extremely tired by the time I got home. About 8 o'clock that evening Phyllis told me that she was feeling funny and that she needed to lie down. At about 11 o'clock that evening she told me that she couldn't explain what was going on with her. Because I was so tired, I told her to go take a shower and come back to bed. She told me that we needed to go to the hospital because she thought that she was going into labor. Because I was expecting that our baby would not be born for another couple of weeks, I was not prepared for the imminent birth of our first child. I got her suitcase and we headed to the car. As soon as she got in the car her water broke and I realized that we needed to get to the hospital immediately. At that time we lived in Riverdale and Northside Hospital was all the way across town. Needless to say I set the land speed record from Riverdale to Northside Hospital.

Around 8 AM on September 26, 1976, Nicholas Joseph Sakas was born. Both he and Phyllis were healthy. When I first saw Nick, I realize that my life had changed forever. It was a deeply spiritual moment. I prayed that I would be able to be a good father and provide for my family. I prayed that I would be able to be a spiritual man and provide spiritual leadership to my family. At that time, I committed myself to Bible study, prayer and fellowship in our church. I undertook to read the Bible from cover to cover and to study the Scripture in a meaningful way. Shortly after Nick's birth I was asked to become a Sunday school teacher and have taught Sunday school continuously since that time. Nick's birth was a spiritually significant part of my life and was as significant to me as when I was first called to be a Christian.

LAW

After I had been with Jesse, Ritchie & Duncan for a few months, Jesse told me that the firm needed me to become involved with representing its main client, United States Fidelity & Guaranty.

That business involved claims of subrogation on behalf of USF&G's construction bond clients. The work entailed becoming involved in construction litigation, one of the most complicated types of litigation in which a young lawyer could get involved. I began going to court on a regular basis on behalf of USF&G throughout the state of Georgia. In one instance, I represented USF&G because it had issued performance bonds to the A. J. Kellos Construction Company. Kellos Construction Company was based in Augusta, Ga. Kellos acted as general contractor on a wide variety of commercial projects. One of the projects was the building of the Houston County Hospital in Perry, Georgia. Houston County is about 40 miles south of Macon.

The hospital was around 98% complete when the heating and air-conditioning subcontractor was completing the installation of a cold-water piping system. On a Friday afternoon in July, the HVAC subcontractor left the cooling system charged, meaning that water was circulating in the system, but had mistakenly forgot to glue one of the PVC pipes together. During the weekend the pipe separated and flooded the hospital. When workers came to the hospital on the following Monday, they opened the door and water came flooding out of the building. Water had gotten into the sheet rock, doors, and cabinetry throughout the mostly completed building and had accumulated in the operating room.

The managing architect, a large architectural firm in Atlanta, condemned all the work that had been previously performed and required that Kellos tear the hospital down and rebuild it. USF&G had issued a performance bond on that project. A performance bond is a guarantee that the contractor will complete the work for which he had contracted in accordance with the plans and specifications for the building in a timely manner. Kellos refused to tear the building down and rebuild it. The owner of the building, Houston County demanded that the hospital be completed on a timely basis. To exasperate the already bad situation, the insurance company that represented the heating and air-conditioning subcontractor, came to the hospital for the purpose of investigating the pending claims against their insured, took hatchets to the sheet rock and destroyed tens of thousands of dollars' worth of the existing walls in the hospital.

Jim Jesse assigned that case to me to investigate and make decisions concerning how the case would be eventually litigated. I began spending a lot of time in Augusta in the Kellos' office and in meetings with Mr. Kellos. One of the major problems that became a big concern early in the litigation was that the water damage had caused an accumulation of mold and mildew throughout the hospital. Summers in Georgia are often hot and humid. Mold and mildew is always problems if too much moisture accumulates in a building. Because this particular building was a hospital the architects excuse for condemning all the work that had been done and requiring the demolition of the entire building and in the subsequent rebuilding of the hospital, was that mold and mildew could cause infections in hospital patients especially if they had wounds or open sores. Mold and mildew can also cause respiratory problems and that was a concern to the architects as well. Kellos, refused to comply with the architects' orders and the hospital authority demanded that the hospital be totally rebuilt. For a few months after the water damage to the hospital all the parties refused to budge from their stated positions. The architects condemned the work and required that the hospital be torn down and rebuilt, Houston County required that the hospital be built on a timely basis, Kellos did not have the resources to tear the building down and restart the building process. USF&G hire my firm and ultimately me to protect its interest as well. My client, USF&G, was not interested in paying for a completely new hospital either. To do that (rebuild a nearly complete hospital all over again) would mean financial ruin to the Kellos Construction Company and would require USF&G to expend great sums of money while it litigated its claims against the HVAC subcontractor. Because USF&G had issued the performance bond on that project it also faced the possibility of having to pay another contractor to demolish and rebuild a $50 million project. USF&G was not excited about that prospect.

After the flooding, the building activities at the hospital stopped and an impasse ensued between Kellos and USF&G on one side and the hospital authority and their architects on the other. The HVAC Company and its insurer was trying to stay neutral or trying to play both sides off the middle. Mold and mildew began to appear in the sheet rock throughout the hospital. The architect's demands to rebuild continued and they issued a condemnation order, meaning that the architect determined that the building that had been almost completed did not meet the plans and specifications and that the work would not be acceptable. To make matters worse,

the HVAC subcontractor was denying responsibility. Kellos did not have sufficient capital in order to
perform any further work as required by the architect and a general standstill regarding the Houston
County hospital prevailed for many months.
Mr. Kellos called me one afternoon to discuss the
problems with the hospital project. We talked about
the mold and mildew problem. The discussion centered on whether the mold and mildew in the damaged walls at the hospital contained pathogens that
could affect potential patients at the hospital. Kellos
had the idea of sending a sample of the mold and
mildew to the biology department at the University of Georgia. It was hoped that the biology department at UGA could determine if there was a manner in which to efficiently remedy the problem of the
mold and mildew. The biology department at UGA
was asked to determine if the mold and mildew had
pathogens that could possibly affect patients receiving treatment at the hospital, and the UGA scientist
were asked to determine how the mold and mildew
should it be treated? Kellos asked for a report from
UGA that would determine if the mold and mildew
could it be treated in such a manner that would be
cost-effective and effectively eliminate the mold and
mildew that was appearing in the walls of the damaged building.

After waiting for about two weeks the chairman
of the biology department at UGA issued a report.
The findings were that the mold and mildew that
was in the samples taken from the Houston County
Hospital were a garden-variety mold that contained
no pathogens that would adversely affect potential
patients at the hospital. The solution recommended
by the university's biology department was that the
walls be treated with Clorox. This was the turning
point of the litigation. However, the end of the litiga-

tion involving the damage to the hospital was still a long way from being finished.

Being the plaintiff in litigation is many times the best position to be in when there are multiple claims to be pursued. The plaintiff can usually control the progress of the case and set the agenda. Being the plaintiff's attorney allows the lawyers to require the defense lawyers to respond to their initiatives. In the hospital case, Kellos and USF&G were subject to being sued by Houston County because the hospital was not timely completed and there were potential problems with various parts of the hospital including a special floor coating that was required in the operating room that would lessen the chance of static electricity adversely affecting operations conducted in that room. Water had gotten into the flooring and had caused water bubbles to appear. Kellos and USF&G also had claims against the HVAC subcontractor for negligent construction and for the damage to the hospital. Lastly, there was a potential claim against the architect for contributing to the delay in the completion of the hospital by issuing a condemnation order that went well beyond what was necessary in order to bring the hospital into substantial completion within the terms of the plans and specifications. USF&G authorized the filing of a lawsuit against the HVAC subcontractor and the architectural firm. USF&G was headquartered in Maryland, the HVAC subcontractor was located in South Georgia and therefore there was complete diversity of citizenship that allowed USF&G to file the case in federal court. I prepared a complaint, traveled to Macon, and filed the case in the United States District Court for the Middle District of Georgia beating the other parties to the courthouse. Therefore, we filed the case in the court that we chose, and we became the plaintiffs.

After suit was filed, the HVAC company third-partied the architectural firm, Heery & Heery into the litigation. The Federal Rules of Civil Procedure provides a method by which a party to the litigation may bring a claim against a non-party contending that that third party is liable to the defendant. By this procedure the additional party can be found to be either fully or partially responsible for the damages that were alleged in the initial lawsuit. In this situation the HVAC company contended that the architectural firm had contributed to the damages that USF&G was alleging in the original lawsuit because the architectural firm had not acted correctly when it condemned the entirety of the hospital. As a result of this tactic there were three sets of lawyers involved in the litigation. USF&G had stepped in to provide financial resources to Kellos to complete the hospital and therefore stepped into Kellos' shoes with regard to the litigation. Even though the interests of USF&G and Kellos were nearly the same with regard to the litigation, Kellos also brought in his own lawyer to monitor the litigation. As it turned out, the problems with the Houston County hospital were not the only problems being encountered by the Kellos Construction Company.

After many months of discovery including many long days of depositions in Augusta and around the state of Georgia, the trial was set for the late fall of 1978. There were many preparations that were necessary in order to be ready to try the case. After spending long hours at the office for several weeks, I finally packed up all the files, got all the documents ready for trial and headed to Macon for the start of the case. I checked into the Hilton Hotel in downtown Macon and happened to run into the opposing counsel, Richard Schultz, in the elevator.

In an effort to intimidate me, Richard looked at me and said, "I'm closing in for the kill."

It just so happened that a convention of hair salon owners was going on in Macon and they were holding their convention in the very same hotel. There was laughter and merriment in the hotel that night and I had a few propositions from strange ladies who had had too much to drink.

Because we had filed as plaintiffs, we were entitled to make the first opening statement. The theme that we chose to alert the jury to the issues in the case was, "your pipe your problem." After months of work, the case boiled down to whether the HVAC company was negligent in failing to glue a pipe that caused water to accumulate in the hospital that was under construction. Interestingly, the pipe in question had had not been produced by the HVAC company when we had subpoenaed its production.

We started the trial without the pipe in question but renewed our motion to compel production of the pipe. Judge Wilber Owen, the trial judge presiding in this case, asked opposing counsel where the pipe was and the HVAC" attorney finally admitted that one of the owners of the HVAC Company had removed the pipe in question and that it was located in Albany in the trunk of the HVAC man's car. Judge Owen told the opposing counsel that the pipe had to be in the courtroom by the following morning. When the pipe arrived, it was still unglued. The judge looked at the opposing counsel and said to him "Mr. Shoolz, I think you need to get your client down here with his check writing machine". At that point in the trial, we believed that we had a very good case and that the case would resolve itself in our favor. The trial lasted for seven trial days and resulted in a verdict in our favor for around $500,000. Additionally, the architectural firm was unable to enforce its condemnation order. Shortly thereafter the hospital was completed and Kellos moved on to other projects.

Cladwood Case

I continued to work on construction cases many of which involved the Kellos Construction Company for the next few years. One interesting case involved an apartment complex in Augusta that was being built by a general contractor from Rome Georgia. In that case, the owner of the project was suing the general contractor because of construction defects. The apartment complex had a brick veneer from the ground to about 6 feet up on the side of the building. Above the brick veneer was a wood-based sheeting made of particleboard called Cladwood that was marketed by the Georgia Pacific Company. That product was manufactured in Oregon and supplied to builders throughout the country.

The apartment complex was having problems with doors not closing properly. Windows were popping out of the side of the building, and the brick row lock at the top of the brick veneer was being pushed downward. The owner of the building insisted that the construction techniques being used by the general contractor was the problem. At first it was very difficult to figure out why the construction was so inadequate. We examined the method by which the Cladwood was nailed to the studs. We even examined the type of wood that was used in the framing of the apartment complex, whether the construction had sufficient venting and whether there was a sufficient moisture barrier between the heated indoor environment and the outside of the construction. Finally, I asked Mr. Kellos to make an examination of the apartment complex to see if he could determine what the problem was. Kellos insisted that we take measurements of the Cladwood siding material. To our amazement we found out that the particleboard was expanding and putting pressure on the brick veneer, windows and doors of the apartment complex. We sent a sample of the particleboard product to the University of Georgia chemistry department to determine the makeup of the resins holding the particleboard together.

In that case the product was a particleboard made up of wood shavings glued together and pressed into the dimensions specified by the manufacturer of the product. The chemical analysis of the particleboard indicated that it was glued together with a resin that was not impervious to water. As a result of this investigation, we brought a third-party complaint against Georgia-Pacific on the theory of products liability. The owner's architect and engineers had specified the Cladwood product in part because it was advertised to be impervious to water. Because the product was specified as being suitable for outdoor applications, it was obvious that the product was not impervious to water and that it did not meet the specifications provided by the supplier of the product. In Georgia, even though the product was not manufactured by Georgia-Pacific, the fact that Georgia-Pacific supplied the product and advertise the product as its own, that fact made Georgia-Pacific libel under the theory of products liability for any defect in the product.

Around Christmas time of that year, I was working on the Cladwood case and had to take a deposition in Eugene, Oregon. I was going to question a representative of the manufacturer of the Cladwood product to find out what he knew about the manufacturing process. It was the first time I had ever flown across the United States. I left from Nashville, Tennessee where we had gone to celebrate the holidays with my parents. I flew to San Francisco and then from San Francisco to Eugene, Oregon. I had never been past Dallas and for the first time I was in a part of the country that was very different. When I disembarked from the airplane in Oregon, I noticed that there were no black people. While that did not bother me, I thought it was very unusual. From the time I was a child living in the southern part of the United States I had always been around black people. Some of the members of my family were members of the KKK but for the most part we were always in close proximity to African Americans and while I did not have any great knowledge about how black people viewed white Americans, I was always intrigued by black culture especially in the South.

After arriving in Eugene, Oregon I had to take a car to the town of Philomath, Oregon. The manufacturer of the Cladwood had a manufacturing plant and we decided to take the deposition of one of the executives of that company. I learned that the Cladwood was made of wood chips and sawdust. The wood shavings were soaked in a resin then pressed into sheets that were approximately 8' x 4' and a half inch thick. The specifications for the Cladwood product that were produced at the deposition required that the product have a phenolic resin that was impervious to water. The use of the product was specified for outside use. That indicated that Cladwood should have been a suitable exterior siding for use in Augusta, Georgia. The tests that we had performed on the Cladwood that was attached to the apartment complex in Augusta indicated that the resin that was used in that particular batch was urea resin. Urea resin is much cheaper than the phenolic resin that was called for in the product specifications and that made that particular batch of Cladwood unsuitable for an exterior siding especially in a hot humid location such as Augusta, Georgia.

On the way back to Atlanta, I had enough time to take a bus from the airport to downtown San Francisco. I remember I carried my suitcase and my briefcase as I walked around a very hilly section of the city by the Bay. I was excited to be in San Francisco, California but I was also excited that I had pieced together not only a good defense to the claims against my client but also had a very good products liability case against Georgia-Pacific. I was anxious to get home to spend the remainder of the Christmas holidays with my family. By then not only were we the parents of Nicholas, but we had also added Alison. Alison was born on June 21, 1979, the first day of summer. She was much smaller than Nick at birth, but it turned out that she was to develop a much larger-than-life personality. While Nick was apprehensive about almost everything, and he tended to hold back, Ali was always full speed ahead. We always had a hard time keeping her from jumping into the pool and from going off on her own to explore. I will always remember seeing her crawling around on the floor and trying to eat whatever was not nailed down. One time, when she was about two, we went to the shopping mall and the moment I took my eye off of her she was in the fountain wadding around. I demanded that she get out of the fountain but to my great displeasure she insisted I come into the fountain to get her. She was just that kind of a child.

Eventually the case involving the apartment complex in Augusta came on for trial in the United States District Court for the Southern District of Georgia, Augusta Division. The case was to be tried in front the Honorable Anthony Alaimo. Judge Alaimo was appointed to the federal bench by President Johnson. During World War II Judge Aliamo became a prisoner of war and it was reported to his wife that he had been killed in action. While he was held prisoner, his wife remarried. When the war was over and he made it back to Georgia, his wife divorced her husband and remarried Judge Alaimo.

Judge Aliamo was a very intense person who absolutely controlled his courtroom. During the pretrial conference the judge insisted that the lawyers meet in order to try to resolve the case by settlement. I worked out a deal with the lawyers representing Georgia-Pacific that was extremely favorable to my clients. We could not work out a suitable agreement with the apartment complex owners but were willing to try that case before a jury. When I announced the settlement of the Georgia-Pacific portion of the case to Judge Alaimo, he insisted that the deal that I had worked out be made available to the apartment complex owners. I told the judge that my client did not want to settle the case against the apartment complex owners. The judge told me that if I did not offer the money that was going to be paid to my client by Georgia-Pacific to the apartment complex owners, then the judge would insist that the president of my client, USF&G, be present in the judge's office on the following morning to explain why the case could not be settled in the manner in which the judge thought best. Needless to say the settlement of the case occurred just as the judge had instructed.

Trouble with the Firm

The law firm, Jesse, Ritchie & Duncan, had expanded and we now had four shareholders and three associates. We were all making a good living and felt as if firm was in a good place. Then a major case was settled, and the firm received a substantial fee. One morning Jim Jesse came into the office and called a firm meeting and announced that he had decided how the money that had been accumulated by the firm would be dispersed. He said that he would take 80% of the money, retire and let us younger guys continue on with the business and pay him a consulting fee.

For the next three months there was an internal fight concerning the split up of the firm. Very little if any client work was accomplished while the members of the firm filed lawsuits against each other. There were three factions in the dispute. Jesse took the position that he owned 70% of the stock of the business and therefore he was entitled to at least 70% of the assets of the corporation if the corporation dissolved. He called a meeting of the shareholders at midnight on a Friday evening expecting that no one would show up for the meeting. To his dismay all of the lawyer showed up and demanded that the meeting be adjourned. Jesse determined to go forward and made a resolution calling for the dissolution of the corporation and a distribution of the corporate assets in accordance with the stock ownership of each shareholder.

Jim Ritchie, me and Walter Beckham formed the second faction. We determined that Jesse had breached his fiduciary duties to the Corporation by using the corporate bank account as his own piggy bank. He paid personal expenses including a new set of tires for his daughter from the corporate account. He paid his personal newspaper subscription from the corporate account and paid all his personal credit card bills from the corporate account. Our position was that because Jesse had breached his fiduciary duty to the corporation that he was not entitled to any distribution from the corporation when it dissolved.

George Duncan decided that it was in his best interests to go forward with his representation of the most prized clients of the corporation, insurance companies. George tried to keep a low profile in the negotiations and in the litigation that followed. As it turned out George's position was probably the better negotiating tactic.

The Jesse faction and what I will call the Ritchie faction wound up hiring counsel to represent each of our respective sides. We wound up in court and had to explain to a Superior Court judge the positions that we were advocating. The judge was amused but did not want to get very involved in a dispute concerning the breakup of the law firm. After each of the sides had a period of time of argument and accusation, we finally all decided to negotiate a final resolution and bring the lawsuit and the law firm to an end. Neither side got everything that they wanted which is often true in negotiated settlements. The best thing that happened was that all the acrimony, vitriol and argument came to an end. Each of the lawyers walked away with something. A few years later I ran into Jim Jesse at the courthouse, and he told me that I had caused him to have a heart attack. That was not true, but it was his last words to me because not too long after that he suddenly died.

I was 32 years old, had been practicing law for seven years, had retained a few cases and was somewhat apprehensive to be out on my own practicing law in Atlanta. I called Fred Cavalli who as you may recall, I had been with when I first came to Atlanta in 1973. Fred was practicing by himself but was in a space sharing situation in an office known as LOL. That name stood for Law Offices Limited, and the acronym was way ahead of its time. There was a wide variety of personalities among those that shared office space at that location. Some of the lawyers that I met at LOL were very colorful. One of the lawyers, Judge Carpenter had been a Superior Court Judge but was forced to retire from the bench when he was accused of attempted murder.

The story that I heard was that Judge Carpenter came home one evening and found his wife in bed with another man. The judge pulled out his pistol and fired a few rounds at the fleeing Paramour. Fortunately, the judge is not a very good shot and by the time the judge had chased his wife's lover down and had him in his sites he had run out of bullets.

One day I was in earshot of a telephone conversation in which Judge Carpenter was telling his client that he needed to pay his fee. Evidently the client did not have sufficient money to bring to the judge that afternoon and the judge told him, "If you do not bring me my fee for your hearing on Monday you will have the shortest trial and the longest sentence of any defendant in the history of Fulton County."

After a few months of being a sole practitioner, Fred and another lawyer, Harold Horne and I decided to form a new law firm. We sat down and drew up an agreement and were going to be partners start-

71

ing the following Monday. When I came to work on the following Monday, I discovered that Fred had moved out of the LOL offices and had joined another law firm. Needless to say, both Harold and I were shocked at that development. Within a few days after the shock had worn off, Harold and I formed a partnership, and we became the firm of Sakas & Horne. Harold and I were the same age. He was from Americus, Georgia. Harold had played football in high school and his high school team had won the state AAA championship. He went to Emory University for his undergraduate degree and then to UGA for law school. Unfortunately, Harold had juvenile onset diabetes that caused him great difficulties throughout his life. Our practice was mostly litigation and we had good success in trying cases together.

Later we expanded to become Whitelaw Sakas & Horne when Bob Whitelaw another one of the LOL alumni joined us. Bob was older and very different from both Harold and me. Bob was from Kansas and drafted into the Army Air Force out of high school during World War II. Bob became a bomber pilot flying missions over Germany when he was only 21 years old. Toward the end of the war his plane was shot down and he wound up in a prisoner of war camp close to Czechoslovakia. When the war was winding down, he and a group of men escaped and wandered around the countryside. Bob said that the prison conditions were so poor that he had lost so much weight that he look like a walking skeleton. While they were wondering around, they happened upon cellar that was full of cheese. Bob said it was the best cheese he had ever eaten. Their group was finally picked up by American GIs and he was returned to the United States. Bob got a job as an insurance adjuster, attended law school and became

72

an attorney in the mid-1950s. Bob was a Baptist and a devout Christian. He had a big influence on my life.

Iliana

During the summer of 1980 I meet Iliana Portik. She was from the Hungarian section of Romania. She grew up in the Transylvania town of Gorginnihi that is located at the corner of the intersection of the Transylvania Alps and the Carpathian Mountains. Her hometown was divided among ethnic Hungarians, Romanians and Gypsies. Ily's first language was Hungarian, but she had to go to first grade in the Romanian school and therefore became fluent in Romanian. Ily was tall and thin and had a very good jump-shot. She was noticed by the Romanian Athletic Association and was groomed to play basketball on their national team. She grew to be 6 feet tall and had big hands and feet for a woman. By the time she was in her early 20s she had played basketball throughout the communist world.

When Ily was a girl, her uncle was able to leave the communist block and immigrate to Toledo, Ohio. Ily planned to escape from Romania and while her team was playing in Italy, she made her escape. She asked for political asylum and was interred in Trieste, Italy. After being in Italy for approximately six months, she was able to convince her uncle in Toledo to sponsor her. She moved to the United States, unable to speak English and without any skills other than her ability to play basketball. Because of her height and because of her unique physical attractiveness, she was striking, and people would immediately notice her when she entered a room. She was often told that she could be a fashion model. One afternoon when she was playing in a pickup game on a playground in Toledo, she was spotted by a man that realize that he could shop her skills to college basketball programs. Middle Tennessee became interested and even though she could speak no English and there were no Hungarian/Romanian language courses she enrolled in college to play basketball at MTSU.

Because my father was the only person available to translate, Ily became a regular fixture at my parent's home in Murphreesboro. In the summer of 1980, I was introduced to Ily when I visited with my parents. I was charmed.

After playing the next season for MTSU, Ily was recruited to play professional basketball in Minnesota. She was not able to make the team and she called me concerning money that she felt was owed to her. The woman's professional basketball league that she was playing in folded shortly thereafter. Ily moved back to Toledo and worked at various jobs trying to support herself. She decided that she wanted to move to Atlanta in order to be closer to me. It wasn't long after that that we became involved romantically.

Things were not going very well between me and Phyllis. Phyllis was very interested in maintaining a very close relationship with her parents and siblings. She was not working, and her time was more and more filled with activities that excluded my participation. Often when I came home from the law office, she turned the children over to my complete control and pursued her own activities. She spent lavishly on gifts for her brother and sisters. One evening I came home to find that Phyllis had planned a dinner party for a church group in which she was involved without telling me. I was left to fend for myself and take care of the children while she engaged in her church activity. Ily became aware of this situation and encouraged me to leave my relationship with Phyllis.

A big regret in my life was when I left my children behind and entered into a new relationship with Ily. The night that I left Phyllis and the children ran counter to my beliefs, however the allure of being in a new relationship with such an exotic person as Iliana was more than I could overcome. In 1982 I divorced Phyllis and took up residence with Ily. I prayed for God's forgiveness and that my children would not suffer for the sins that I had committed.

I had been working on a case involving a manufacturing company from Bilboa, Spain. The company manufactured machines that made screws and headers on bolts. Their machines were of a unique design and were being marketed in the United States. One of the Spanish company's creditors seized two of their machines while there were at a tradeshow in Atlanta. Prejudgment attachment can be accomplished in certain limited instances especially when it is likely that the property subject to attachment will be taken out of the jurisdiction of the court unless it is seized. While I was working on that case, I decided that it was necessary to visit my client in Spain. Except for going across the border at Niagara Falls I had never been out of the United States. Ily wanted to visit relatives in Budapest, so we decided to take a two-week trip to Spain and other points of interest in Europe.

We flew on Lufthansa to Frankfurt, Germany and had a long layover there. We then took an Iberia Air flight to Bilbao. We were met by my client and taken to a hotel because we were exhausted from our travel. The next morning, I got up and went out on the street in front of the hotel and realized that I was in a whole different place. I went into the restaurant and realized that I could not order anything because I did not speak any Spanish. People at the table next to me were close enough for me to hear what they were saying, and I was able to mimic their order by saying in Spanish, "Café con leche con tostada". Soon the waiter brought me a cup of coffee with milk and an order of toast with jelly. I felt very proud of myself for being able to at least order coffee and toast. Ily spoke Romanian fairly well. Romanian is somewhat related to Italian and therefore she was able to also speak a little Spanish. We navigated through the city that morning and were able to get her some breakfast and do a little sightseeing.

Later that evening my client picked us up and took us to dinner at a fairly expensive restaurant. My experience with the Spanish people in Bilbao was that they made me feel welcome and enforced my feeling that I could communicate in an effective way with people of a different culture. After visiting the factory and being escorted around the surrounding countryside by my client, Ily and I flew to Madrid again on Iberia Air. Our flight had a smoking and a non-smoking section. In the United States the smoking section on the airplane was in the back. On Iberia Air the smoking section was on the right. I never really understood the rationality of that smoking and non-smoking section. We spent the night in Madrid and the next morning rented a Fiat Uno, a car that was little bit larger than a roller-skate and begin a road trip that would eventually take us as far east as Budapest.

We traveled Northeast across a high plain that seemed very arid. By the time we got to Zaragoza, Ily and I had had a fight and we were not speaking. I stopped the car on a downtown street and found a grocery market. I bought cheese, bread, a bottle of wine and water. In Spain water comes with carbonation or without carbonation (con gasses or sine gasses). After we had eaten, we were back on speaking terms and proceeded from Zaragoza to Barcelona. Along the way, Ily insisted that the farmers of that region did not mind sharing from their fruit trees as we passed peach orchards. She insisted that I stop the car so that she could get out and allow the farmers to share their fruit. Prior to traveling to Spain I had read James Michener and had also read Hemingway's *For Whom the Bells Toll*, just to get a sense of some of the history and locations. I found Michener's Iberia, while somewhat dated, to be very helpful in understanding the culture of Spain.

By the time we came close to Barcelona it was already getting dark and we decided to drive a little further and stopped at Gerona, a town on the Costa Brava. We found a hotel room and could hear people partying most of the night. In the morning we had toast and coffee and drove to the beach. It was the first time I had ever seen a beach full of women going topless as a matter of normality. We continued driving towards the frontier between Spain and France. The scenery was absolutely beautiful. The Pyrenees Mountains fell right into the Mediterranean. The mountains against the very blue waters as we meandered along a very winding coastal road, was spectacular. We stopped at a store, bought some more groceries and had a picnic on a rock that gave us a perfect view of the sea.

Later in the afternoon we got to the French border and crossed into France without any incident. We soon found a place where we could walk down a long flight of stairs to the beach. We decided to dip our feet in the Mediterranean. When we got to the bottom of the staircase we looked over to the right and there was a couple making love. Our presence did not seem to bother them, and we got a good look at some of the local scenery. We drove on and Ily insisted that the local grape growers were also good about sharing their fruit with perfect strangers such as us. We came to the town of Nardonne and continued to drive out to the beach. We could not get a hotel room there, so we drove back towards the interstate highway. We passed another vineyard and Ily insisted that we stop so that the farmer could share. She got out of the car and started towards the vineyard when she heard the barking of a very large dog. She returned to the car and glibly said she did not think that farmer was in a sharing mood.

We finally made it to Montpellier very late in the evening. We found a hotel that was open, and I told Ily that she should go in and see if she could get a room for us. She had studied French, and I felt that she could speak enough French to get us a room for the evening. She got out of the car, and I picked up the luggage and followed her. She got to the hotel desk and rang the bell. A man came through a beaded glass doorway. Ily looked at the man and said in perfect English, "do you speak French?" The man rubbed his eyes looked at her and said again in perfect English, "yes I speak French, but I also speak English." We got a room and I believe that the last person who stayed in that room could have been Napoleon himself. The closet was a hook on the wall, and the pillow was chained to the bed. The bathtub was the type that had legs, and the showerhead was in the middle of the wide side of the tub. The towels felt more like bedsheets. When we got into bed, both of us rolled to the middle, not because we wanted to be in close contact but because the bed was so old that it sagged, and it caused everything including us to roll towards the middle.

The next morning, we got up and went down to the restaurant for what is known as continental breakfast. There was coffee and bread. After I had sat at the table for a few minutes another couple walked in with a very large dog. Dogs always liked me and this one was no exception. He came right over sat on the floor and placed his head on the table next to my food. Evidently, people in France love their dogs so much that they insist on taking them into restaurants.

Later that day we made it to Marseille. I had seen the movie, *The French Connection* and recognized the harbor area from the movie. We had lunch of bouillabaisse and then drove on to Nice by way of Cannes. When we came into Nice it was late afternoon. We stopped the car near the beach and decided to walk along the beach in order to stretch our legs. Again, ladies do not wear tops on their bathing suits on the Riviera. Ily noticed that I was getting an eye full of the young ladies on the beach, and she was keeping me in line by holding onto my arm as we walked. The next thing I knew she had walked me right into a telephone pole and said she did it so that I would not trip over my tongue. The next day we went out onto the beach, but she refused to go topless. The beach was full of small round stones and the water was frigid. Later that day we traveled through the Alps on our way to the Italian town of Torrin, which is known as Torino by the Italians. While I was driving Ily continued to brush up on her Italian because she had friends in Torino that we wish to visit.

Driving in Italy is an experience. Drivers often ride with the driver side window open so that they can yell at other drivers and make obscene gestures. We arrived in Torino and got in contact with Ily's friend Carlotta. Carlotta had helped Ily when she defected from the Romanian basketball team. Carlotta and Ily were happy to see each other and reminisced about basketball and Ily's escape. We stayed in Torino for a few days and one morning I decided that I would go to see the Shroud of Turin. Unfortunately, the exhibit was closed, and I had to settle for going to the museum of Egyptology. In that museum there was an exhibit on the Rosetta Stone and because I did not speak or read Italian, I was under the impression that the Rosetta Stone was at that museum. It turned out that it was only a replica with the original Rosetta Stone being in London. We met other people that Ily had dealt with in Torino and were reluctant to leave but we had decided to see other sites.

We left Torino and drove across northern Italy. We made a quick stop in Milano. Ily had been taking courses at Georgia State University and was studying graphic design. She had met a student there and he had gotten a job in Milano working with the fashion designer Gianni Versace. While we were in Milano, we were able to visit Gianni Versace's studio which was located in his mansion. Later that evening we arrived at the outskirts of Venice. We found a car park, put the car down and took a taxi boat to the city.

There is nothing like Venice. We wandered around, had a pleasant dinner and became hopelessly lost. In order to get back to our car before the car park closed for the evening, we had to get back on the boat by 10 o'clock. Because we had gotten lost, we could not find the place where we needed to get back on the boat to get to our car. We had no idea how much money we had on hand because we had left our travelers checks in our luggage in the car. Finally, Ily insisted that we go into a hotel. She went into the lady's room and returned with a $100 bill that she had pinned into her bra. We changed the Ben Franklin into lira, and we got directions to a cab stand. We were able to make our way back to the car park. When we got there everything was locked down. We had to climb the fence to get to our car. We wound up spending the night sleeping in the car. The next morning when the attendant arrived, we were ready to drive out. I think we really confused the attendant.

Trieste was the next place that we decided to visit. After finding a hotel along the auto via, we were able to wash our faces change our underwear and have a small breakfast. Trieste is in the northeast corner of Italy very close to what was then the border of Yugoslavia. When Ily escaped from the Romanian basketball team she was interred at a government facility in Trieste. There she met Alex, another Romanian who had escaped and who was also being processed at the government facility in Trieste. Eventually Alex settled in Montréal. Alex had been on the Romanian rugby team and eventually he became the director of the workout facilities at the Stadium Olympic in Montréal.

Our goal was to travel to Budapest, so we crossed from Italy into Yugoslavia. We changed the lira that we had accumulated into dinars, the Yugoslavian currency at that time. We traveled through very picturesque mountains that eventually led us through the town of Zagreb. We drove on roads with very little traffic. At that time there was a divided highway, but the road only had one lane on each side of the divide. I needed to take a bathroom break and there was a sign that indicated that there was a rest stop ahead. I pulled off the road into the parking lot and went through a gate that I thought would lead me to the men's room. It actually led me to a field that had high grass and I could see places that had toilet paper. In other words, the restroom was nothing more than a grassy spot where one could do their business in relative privacy. We traveled on.

As late afternoon approached, we became hungry and thirsty. We came into a small town not far from the Hungarian border and decided that we would have a rest stop and see if we could get something to eat. We went into a saloon that looked somewhat like what is pictured in old Western movies. There was a swinging door entrance just like the one at the long branch in the television series Gunsmoke. There was a group of men sitting playing dominoes and a very thick cloud of cigarette smoke in the air. We went to the bar and tried to communicate as best we could that we were hungry and wanted to eat. The bartender did not speak any of the languages that we spoke. We tried Hungarian, Romanian, French, Italian and Russian. The bartender replied in Serbian and in German. Finally by hand motions we were able to communicate that we wanted to eat and drink. Soon a waitress brought us a couple bottles of beer and a plate of sausages with tomatoes and onions. At that point I became worried because I had no idea of how much money we had in dinars. When the waitress brought the bill, I pulled all the Yugoslavian money I had in my pocket out and put it on the table. The waitress took the smallest amount of money, and everybody left happily.

We arrived at the Hungarian border just after dark. At that time Hungary was still in the eastern bloc of countries and had a communist form of government. After about an hour's delay while the border guards looked us over, we crossed into Hungary and drove a short distance to a town on the shore of Lake Balaton. We found a youth hostel, got a room without a bathroom in it and settled in for the evening. After getting in bed, Ily rolled over on top of me and whispered in my year, "welcome to the land of your forefathers." I felt very welcomed indeed and slept very soundly that evening.

The next morning when we got up, I could smell sausage cooking at a restaurant close to where we were staying. After breakfast we drove to Budapest. We approached that great city from the west and first came to the village of Budha-Kessie. It turned out that Ily had an aunt and an uncle that lived in that village. Lusica Neni (Aunt Louise) and her husband Jonchie Bacsi (Uncle John) lived on a hillside and were home when we arrived. There were no phones for us to call ahead and we had to explain who we were and where we were from, but there were very happy to see us and immediately took us in and wanted to party. We walked down to the local bor pincer (wine cellar), and they ordered a gallon of very sweet white wine. We sat on a picnic table and began to knock this wine back. Before long we were joined by Gero Bacsi (Uncle Gene), and he invited us over to his house to continue the party. After everyone was sufficiently lubricated, they all began to sing. At first, they would sing happy songs, and everyone would laugh and giggle. Then they would sing very sad songs, and everyone would begin to cry. This went on for what seemed like all night long. By the time we made it back to Lusica Neni's house we were all stumbling.

The next morning, as you would expect, I had a very bad hangover. Evidently the treatment for hangover in Hungry is to have more to drink. I just couldn't bring myself to drink a beer for breakfast, so I decided to go for a walk. I finally found a Catholic Church at the bottom of the hill and went in just to sit and clear my head. I thought of my need for prayer and prayed that we would make it back to Atlanta. After my head cleared, we drove across the Danube to the Pest side of Budapest. We found the apartment where Maresca Neni and Lutzy Bacsi lived. Fortunately, they were also at home and invited us to spend the night. That side of the family did not insist that we drink ourselves into oblivion but were equally happy to see us and wanted to know all about our lives in America. Their apartment was three floors up and there was no elevator. The next morning, I walked down to the street and there were men making repairs to the elevator. It was around 9:30 in the morning and they were taking their morning break. The morning break consisted of drinking wine and smoking cigarettes.

Maresca Neni's mother also lived with the family. She had been in Budapest during the fighting that occurred there during World War II. I asked her how things were during that time. She said that when the Germans came into town that they stole all the good stuff that they could put on their trucks. She also said that when the Russians came through town, they took everything including bathroom fixtures and even the pipes in the walls.

We left Budapest and drove back through Austria and arrived in Munich, Germany. Ily's roommate from college who also played on the Romanian national team with Ily lived in Munich with her husband. They had a condo on the fifth floor of a fairly modern building. They owned a small business in which they supplied computers to other small businesses. I gave her husband a Palm Pilot for which he was very grateful. We were invited to spend the next few days with Diana and her husband Johanos. We explored Munich and had a wonderful time visiting with Diana and her husband.

We drove from Munich to Frankfurt, put the car down and flew back to Atlanta. My first trip to Europe as you can tell from reading this was very memorable and gratifying. I will never forget driving from Madrid across Spain, seeing the French Riviera, traveling to Turin and Venice traveling through Yugoslavia and especially my first night in Hungry.

The Brown Reality Cases

When we got back to Atlanta, Bob Whitelaw asked me to get involved in a case in which his client, Annie Thomas who was being evicted from her house. Annie lived in the West End area of Atlanta on Beecher Street. She had lived in her house for 20 years. Annie Thomas worked as a forklift driver in a warehouse over on Fulton Industrial Boulevard. She got behind on her mortgage and was threatened with foreclosure. Annie had approximately $25,000 of equity in her house and was afraid that after the many years that she had lived there she would be without a roof.

Georgia is a non-judicial foreclosure state, which means that the mortgage company or the lender that holds a security interest in real property (real estate) can initiate a foreclosure proceeding and sell the property at auction without going before a judge. In other words there is no one to determine whether the foreclosure procedure has been followed correctly and on many occasions the foreclosure process is subject to abuse. Bob Whitelaw asked me to become involved with the specific aspects of the foreclosure process regarding Annie Thomas's house.

In Georgia and in about half the other states, the mortgage company must notify the debtor in writing that they are behind on their payments, notify the debtor in writing that if the debtor does not bring the debt current that a foreclosure will occur on the first Tuesday of the following month between the hours of 10:00 AM and 4:00 PM. The creditor must also advertise the notice of foreclosure in the legal newspaper of the county in which the property is located. Because Georgia and many other states allow non-judicial foreclosures, the process is subject to abuse.

When Annie Thomas got behind on her mortgage and it was advertised in the legal newspaper, Annie was contacted by Al Brown. Al and his parents Alonzo and Gladys were the principles of the Brown Realty Company. The Browns had embarked on a scheme in which they would contact individuals like Annie Thomas who were subject to a foreclosure notice and who had large amounts of equity in their homes. Al came to Annie's house and told her that his mom, Gladys, was a good person and that she wanted to help Annie save her house. Al told Annie that Gladys would loan her the money to catch up her mortgage and that Annie could repay the Browns over time. Annie agreed that she needed Gladys Brown's help and believed that the Browns would help her save her house.

Al Brown took Annie Thomas to the office of Jeffrey Kneller, a lawyer, in Decatur, for the purpose of signing papers in order to "help" Annie Thomas "save her house". Annie Thomas had minimal education and while she could read did not understand the documents that she was asked to sign. Annie was told that the documents that she was signing was for a loan from Gladys Brown to Annie and that the money would be paid to the mortgage company on behalf of Annie.

Instead, Annie signed a quitclaim deed transferring ownership of her property to Gladys Brown. She signed a closing statement in which she received less than $100 in cash for transferring her house to the Browns. She also signed a lease in which she agreed to pay monthly rent to the Browns to allow her to stay in her house. Within a few months the

Browns filed a dispossessory warrant in The State Court of Fulton County in order to evict Annie Thomas from her home.

Annie Thomas contacted Bob Whitelaw to answer the dispossessory. Bob asked me to get involved in Annie Thomas's representation. He asked me to come up with a cause of action to protect Annie's property rights. A year or so before I had assisted Fred Cavalli in a case in Clayton County against a company called Payday Motors. In that case a used car salesman had sold the car to a little old lady and required that she make weekly payments for the car at the car dealership. The dealership required that she have insurance on the car and when they determined that she did not have enough insurance they repossessed her car. A man dressed in a sheriff's uniform came to her door after 11:00 PM and demanded that our client turn the car over to him. It turned out that the man's name was Sheriff, but he was not the Sheriff and did not work in the Sheriff's office. Fred sued Payday Motors on the theory of fraud, and I became familiar with Georgia case law dealing with fraudulent transactions. We also sued Payday Motors on the theory of violation of the Georgia Fair Businesses Practices Act. Fred won the case. The only trouble in that case was that we did not ask for enough money in damages. The jury was incensed and would have awarded almost any amount that we would have asked for.

Annie Thomas had been lied to by the Browns and they needed to pay. Not only Annie, but there were other individuals in the same situation as Annie. The others had the same representations made to them by the Browns and thus became involved in the Brown's scheme. By representing Annie, we were also learning how to help others that had been affected by the foreclosure abuse that the Browns were perpetrating

Fraud consists of five elements: 1) a representation is made by the defendant, the Browns, to the plaintiff, Annie Thomas; 2) the representation is false at the time that it is made; 3) the defendant knows that the representation is false at the time that the representation is made (this particular element of fraud is also referred to as scienter, a term meaning "having guilty knowledge and intent" to do wrong); 4) the plaintiff could not have known that the representation was false when it was made; 5) the plaintiff is damaged as a result of the false representation. In addition, Georgia law requires that the plaintiff use reasonable diligence in order to determine whether the representation was false at the time that it was made. When Al Brown made his representations to Annie Thomas, they were false. Al told Annie that Gladys Brown wanted to help her save her ownership interest in her house. Instead, the Browns wanted to acquire Annie's ownership interest so that they could strip the equity that Annie had built up over the years in her house. When Annie was taken to Jeffrey Kneller's law office instead of signing loan documents, Annie was required to sign a quitclaim deed transferring ownership of her property to the Browns. Annie then signed a lease obligating her to pay rent to the Browns if she wanted to remain in possession of her house. These misrepresentations were made by the Browns with the intent of divesting Annie of her ownership interest in her house and for the purpose of allowing the Browns to obtain a loan from NationsBank to strip the equity in Annie's house. As I mentioned earlier Annie Thomas had approximately $25,000 of equity in her house meaning that the value of the house exceeded what she owed by $25,000.

An additional cause of action similar to fraud is a cause of action under the civil provisions of the Georgia Racketeer Influenced and Corrupt Organization Act, also known as the RICO act. RICO requires that the plaintiff prove that the defendant has committed either directly or indirectly a series of criminal acts, also referred to as predicate acts, that has affected (damaged) the plaintiff's property including money. The RICO act also requires that the plaintiff prove that the series of acts has occurred within five years of the time in which the last act occurred. In Annie Thomas's case the predicate act that she was basing her RICO claim on was that of Theft by Deception. Theft by deception is closely related to fraud but does not require that the victim of the theft use reasonable care to prevent the theft. In other words, if the perpetrator of the theft by deception is able to acquire property or money from the victim the victim does not have to be aware and take measures to prevent the crime.

Soon after I got involved in the Annie Thomas matter other victims of the Brown's scheme to acquire their property began to call us for the purpose of also representing their interests. When all was said and done, we represented 13 individuals that had very similar stories concerning how their houses were also acquired by the Browns after they had been given foreclosure notices by their mortgage companies. We were also contacted by The Atlanta Legal Aid Society because they also had individuals that were impacted by the Browns scheme. I decided that we should try to represent all of the victims of the Browns scheme by filing a class-action lawsuit based on fraud and violations of the Georgia civil RICO act. (There is also a federal RICO statute, a discussion of that statute will occur later when I relate the case against Fleet Finance Company).

Annie's case was filed in the Superior Court of DeKalb County and was assigned to Judge Clarence Seeliger. Judge Seeliger had become a judge in DeKalb County by running against J. Oscar Mitchell who had put Martin Luther King Jr. in jail in the 1960s. It was that incident that caused Bobby Kennedy who later became the Attorney General of the United States to obtain Dr. King's release. Judge Seeliger had also been involved in the Presidential Parkway cases in which my good friend and neighbor Susan Garrett was seeking to prevent the use of several parks running along Ponce de Leon Avenue from being turned into the presidential Parkway after the building of the Jimmy Carter Presidential Library. Susan was successful in preventing the use of the parks and an alternate Parkway was built linking downtown Atlanta to the Carter library.

I had been involved in a potential class-action when I was still working at Jesse Ritchie & Duncan. We had filed an action on behalf of a client against C&S National Bank in Fulton County. I was working with Walter Beckham one of the associates on behalf of Jackie Fechskin's who had placed the settlement proceeds from her husband's wrongful death in trust with C&S bank. C&S manipulated the trust funds in order to bail out risky investments it had made in its REIT (real estate investment trust). While we were working on that case, we thought about filing a class-action and had discussed class actions with an attorney from a large firm in Washington DC who met us in Atlanta and gave us a day long introduction regarding the procedures for filing and maintaining a class action. Based on that tutorial regarding what was required to be proven in class-action litigation it was my belief that Annie Thomas' case against the Browns met the criteria for maintaining a class-action.

In order to maintain a class-action there are six elements of proof that the plaintiff is required to provide to the court. First there must be what is referred to as numerosity. Numerosity means that there are a sufficient number of individuals that are involved in order to make the action economically feasible. Generally there must be more than 25 individuals who would qualify as plaintiffs so that the joining of each of the plaintiffs would make it difficult to proceed. Secondly, the plaintiff must prove that there is a common set of facts or legal principles that affects each of the plaintiffs. This is generally referred to as commonality. Thirdly, there is the issue of typicality. Typicality means that the claims of the named plaintiff are similar in most respects to the claims of all of the other unnamed plaintiffs. Fourthly, the plaintiff must meet the criteria of having a representative capacity. Representative capacity means that the named plaintiff does not have any adverse interest to the unnamed class members that would prevent the named plaintiff from acting in a representative capacity. Fifthly, the attorneys representing the named plaintiff must have sufficient experience in handling complex litigation to make it feasible for them to represent the entire class in that particular litigation. Sixthly, the plaintiff must demonstrate that the use of the class-action is a superior method of handling the litigation.

We submitted our petition for class certification to Judge Seeliger and he certified the case as a class-action. The defendants appealed the certification order to the Georgia Supreme Court. The Supreme Court based on an opinion that had been rendered in the 11th Circuit Court of Appeals determined that class actions could not be based upon the theory of fraud and therefore reversed certification order. Later the Supreme Court would reverse its position concerning whether a class-action based on fraud could be certified.

When the case was returned to the Superior Court of DeKalb County, all sorts of motions were filed including a motion for the Browns to be held in contempt of court for tampering with potential clients. At one hearing, when everyone had their backs turned, Al Brown made a threatening gesture to me indicating that he was going to cut my throat. Gladys Brown was held in contempt of court and incarcerated for a few days.

Finally, the case was ready for trial and a jury was impaneled and testimony started. I noticed that there was a strange woman sitting in the courtroom while the case was being tried and found out that the Browns had hired a "root lady" to cast a spell on me during the trial. While the case was being tried, I was assisted by Bill Brennan at the Atlanta Legal Aid Society who provided needed testimony concerning the pattern of criminal activities engaged in by the Browns. The case was finally turned over to the jury who returned a verdict in Annie Thomas's favor in the amount of $350,000. Everyone associated with the case was very happy with the outcome. The Browns appealed to the Georgia Court of Appeals. The Georgia Court of Appeals upheld the verdict and we established very good legal authority for the handling of similar cases. In other words we were successful in helping not only Annie Thomas but a whole group of people who had been harmed by the Browns.

Products Liability

While I was working on the Annie Thomas case I was contacted by Yehuda Smolar, an attorney who I had known from the time I was with Jesse, Richie & Duncan. Yehuda had gotten a case involving two young sailors who had been injured in an automobile wreck while driving from Cherry point North Carolina to Jacksonville, Florida. The driver of the car Gary Hardison was an exceptional young man who had joined the Navy after high school. Gary taught himself how to read music and was able to play several musical instruments without formal instruction. Gary could also speak Chinese. He and two other young sailors were driving down I-95 between Savannah and Brunswick when the rear passenger side tire blew out. The car went into a slide, started to roll and Gary was ejected, and his body came to rest on the road surface. Danny, a passenger in the back smashed his head into the rear window that cause the entire scalp of his head to be torn off.

Yehuda asked me and my then partner, Harold Horne, to take Danny's case but co-operate with Yehuda in the discovery related to Gary's case. We decided that there was a defect in the rear suspension of the Ford Escort automobile that was being driven by Gary and in which Danny was the passenger. We were able to recover the left rear strut from the Escort. Upon physical examination of that strut it was evident that the metal mounts, that attach the strut to the wheel, had torn in a manner that was obviously not intended by the manufacturer. I had become involved in trying products liability cases since the time that I had taken the case in Augusta involving the Georgia-Pacific/ Cladwood product that I discussed earlier. Under Georgia law if you can

95

prove that a product is defective and that the product caused the injury to the individual using that product then the law determines that the manufacture the product is strictly liable. Sometimes products liability cases are referred to as strict liability cases. In the case involving Gary and Danny we believed that the rear suspension system on the 1983 Ford Escort being driven by Gary was defective.

I started studying the geometry of the rear suspension of the Ford Escort. The strut assembly was attached at a 45° angle from the frame of the Escort to the wheel. We hired several experts to help us understand how the geometry of the suspension system could cause the Escort to roll over. We determined that the angle of the strut caused a jacking affect as the car slid. In other words, the angle of the strut assembly acted almost like a pole vault so that when the car went into a slide and the tire was dragged along the surface of the road that event had the same effect as a pole vaulter sticking his pole into the box at the end of the runway. The force that would be exerted on the angled members of the suspension of the car would cause a lifting affect (depending upon the angle in which the poll was inserted into the box). Of course, Ford disputed our theory and we prepared for trial before Judge Orinda Evans of the United States District Court for the Northern District of Georgia. Just prior to trial Harold had become very involved with the strut that had been taken from the 1983 Escort. The metal was torn in a particular direction and after sitting and staring at the way the metal was torn, he had an epiphany that was very helpful in solving the question of the geometry of the rear end of the car that became very important in the presentation of the case.

The case took eight trial days to present to the jury. During the trial Ford insisted that it be allowed to put into evidence an exemplar of the strut in question. I argued strongly against the introduction of the exemplar but eventually Judge Evans allowed the evidence to be submitted to the jury.

Gary's injuries were dramatic. He suffered from a brain injury when his head hit the concrete on the interstate. Gary stayed in the Navy hospital in Jacksonville for an extended period of time. He lost the ability to walk without severe impairment and also lost some of his ability to speak. We had experts testify concerning his abilities to become gainfully employed as a result of his injuries.

The jury stayed out for approximately five hours and returned a verdict in our favor in the amount of $1,750,000. After the jury was dismissed the foreman of the jury came up to me to congratulate me on the presentation of the case. He told me that I was a "sly dog" for allowing the exemplar of the strut to be put into evidence because he said the jury had been looking at the actual strut as compared to the exemplar and was able to determine that the actual strut was defective. I did not have the heart to tell him that I had argued against allowing the exemplar to be put into evidence. You never know what will cause a jury to make a decision. All you can do is put the evidence before them and hope for the best.

After we tried the Annie Thomas case, we still had 11 other clients that had claims against the Browns. We proceeded to get those cases ready for trial and eventually were able to obtain verdicts totaling $3,500,000. In order to escape paying the judgments against them, the Browns decided to transfer all of their assets to a woman (probably a relative) in

South Carolina. When we discovered that the Browns were divesting themselves of all their assets, we filed a claim of receivership before Judge Seeliger. Judge Seeliger granted our request for receivership and ordered that the Brown's divest themselves of their assets. We were able to take control of approximately 80 houses and 25 mortgages owned by the Browns. We also were able to recover some cash. The receiver tried to liquidate the property over an extensive period of time to no avail. As a last resort the receiver deeded houses and mortgages to my clients and to me for my fee and handling the case.

Iliana's Family

My divorce from Phyllis was final in November 1981. Ily and I started living together and on May 22, 1982, we got up that morning walked from our apartment on North Avenue to the Fulton County Courthouse, found the chaplain and got married. A few weeks later we took a train trip from Atlanta to Boston. We rented a car and drove to Cape Town and enjoyed a respite from the heat of Atlanta while it was still cool in New England. After a few months of living together we found a condo in Decatur. The following spring, we invited Ily's mother and brother, Josey, to visit us. Neither one of them had ever been out of Romania nor had they ever flown. When we finally picked them up at the Atlanta airport each one had a small suitcase with nothing but a change of underwear. They were very excited and had never seen the kind of houses that are prevalent along Ponce de Leon Avenue. Ily's mother who I will refer to as Anya which is Hungarian for mother wanted to know if the houses were schools or hospitals.

That evening we sat on our patio after dinner and neither Josey, Ily's brother, nor Anya would talk above a whisper. We asked them why they would not speak up and they replied that you did not know who was listening. At that time the Romanian government was controlled by the family of the dictator Ceausescu and the secret police. The secret police listened to most conversations, continually monitored phone calls and continually threatened people who expressed dissatisfaction with the government.

A few days later Ily took her mother to the grocery store. Anya was amazed at the variety of groceries. She told Ily that we should buy 200 pounds of sugar and store it in the attic of our condo. Ily asked her mother why we should do that, and Anya replied that the sugar might not be there the next time they went to the store. Ily assured her mother that the sugar would be there the next time they went to the grocery. Later, when we traveled to Romania, I began to understand why Anya was so concerned. In the Romanian grocery stores, there were only sardines and vodka. In order to get bread, you had to stand in a long line at the bakery. The Romanians had no sugar, no coffee, nor other products that we would take for granted.

We decided that while Anya and Josey were staying with us that we would have a church wedding. We invited our friends and my family, set up the wedding at the church that we attended and had a ceremony so that Anya could see that her only daughter was a beautiful bride and that she was legally married. We had the reception at our condo. So many of our friends and family attended the reception that our condo was overflowing with people. Ily did all the cooking and made the wedding cake. We had plenty of champagne and a great time was had by all. Later that afternoon Ily and I escaped from the crowd and we made love and cemented our marriage.

Travels in Romania

Later that year we decided to go to Romania. Prior to leaving Atlanta Ily asked me to go to the drug store and buy two cartons of Kent cigarettes and big boxes of condoms. When I got home with those items Ily said that it was not enough and sent me back to the drugstore to get the same amount of cigarettes and condoms again. The lady at the cash register was the same lady that checked me out on my first trip to the drugstore and she was very impressed, thinking that I had gone through all the cigarettes and condoms in just a few hours.

In September 1987 we flew to Budapest, rented a car and drove eastward towards the Romanian border. We got about halfway to the border when we realize that we had been so excited that we left our luggage at the airport in Budapest. We turned around and headed back towards the airport. When we got into the city of Szolnok we were stopped by the local police because I had been speeding. The policeman told us that it was going to be expensive and told us that it was going to cost us one red one. At that time the Hungarian currency was forints and a red one was 500 forints. I quickly did the calculation and realize that the fine was approximately eight dollars in American money. We quickly paid the policeman and finally got back to the airport and retrieve our bags. We again headed for the town of Barretyofaol which was on the Hungarian side of the border with Romania. We stayed there that night in a home that was approved for guests. It was a precursor to an Airbnb way before there was such thing as an Airbnb. In the morning we got up and went to the first grocery store we could find and loaded up the car with the groceries that we bought. We bought out the store's supply of coffee, sugar, and Pepsi, the preferred soft drink in Romania.

We arrived at the Romanian border in late morning. There was a long wait while the Romanian border guard inspected our luggage, required us to change money, and just made us wait around for the pleasure of seeing us wait. Finally, Ily decided she would offer a couple of packs of Kent cigarettes to the border guard and immediately the gate opened, and we were able to enter Romania.

At that time there were no road maps available for anyone driving through Romania. There were very few road signs and unless you knew your way through the country it was very difficult to navigate. The first town that we headed for was Oradea, a large town close to the Danube River. As we were entering the city a sheepherder herded his sheep across the road and we had to wait until the sheep cleared before we could proceed. When we got into the city and stopped at a stoplight a group of young boys rushed our car tried to open all the doors and stick their hands through the windows. Fortunately, all the doors were locked, and the windows were up, or they would have stolen everything that was in the car.

From Oradea we headed north towards Cluj. Cluj is the second largest city in Romania and while Ily was still in high school she was sent to Cluj to start her preparation for playing on the Romanian national basketball team. It was in Cluj that she began her friendship with Diana. They both played on the same college team and later became teammates on the national team. From Cluj we finally found the road to Turga-Moruish an industrial town that was home to Ily's godmother and godfather. We got there and found their apartment but neither of them was at home. Ily's godmother's son Andrus happened to be there and as it turned out wanted to travel with us on to Gorginnihi, Ily's hometown. Fortunately for us he knew the route and we started our drive to Ily's hometown that afternoon. We traveled a few miles, and all the traffic was stopped. It turned out that a train was crossing the road ahead of us. In Romania, traffic stops 20 minutes before the train arrives and is not allowed to proceed until 10 minutes after the train has gone by.

While we were sitting there waiting for the train to go bye, I asked Andrus what work he did. He said that he worked at the funeral home washing bodies in preparation for their burial. I remarked that that seemed to be a very depressing job. Andrus became very serious and finally, he said, "no he was very happy to have the job". Andrus told us that earlier that year he had been arrested for not having a job. After he and his wife had broken up, he had been fired for missing work from a local contracting company. Evidently in Romania it is illegal to be unemployed. Andrus said while he was in jail, he was beaten almost every day and that impressed to him of the necessity of having a job, even if the job was working in a morgue preparing bodies for burial.

We arrived in Ily's hometown in early evening. We stopped at the downtown area for Ily to get her bearings. While we were stopped, she got out and tried to get someone to give her directions to her brother's house. I was standing outside of the car and was approached by a person who was obviously a Gypsy. The Gypsy was begging me to give him a bar of soap. I was reluctant to dig around in our luggage but based upon his appearance I thought it was okay to open the car and look through the luggage to find a bar of soap. Because I was downwind of the stranger that was demanding a bar of soap from me, I realized his need and came up with the bar of soap to present to him with the hope that he would soon use it. He was very appreciative. Later I found out that the chief of the all the local Gypsies was a man by the name of Patchko. Mr. Patchko was extremely ugly, but he insisted that he was the most beautiful man in the world and everyone else was ugly in comparison to him. A night or two later I saw Patchko riding his horse up and down the main street in Gorginnihi, leaning from side to side in the saddle and he was obviously drunk as a skunk.

After dropping off Andrus we finally arrived at Josey's house and settled in for the evening. His house was surrounded by a large yard and a high fence. Within the fenced area there was an extensive garden, several fruit trees, an outhouse and an area where his wife Augi raised rabbits. Augi kept rabbits for meat and for their hides. The reason that the fence was so high was because the Gypsies lived in their own encampment not far from Josey's house. I noticed that all the houses on that street also had high fences and was told that it was necessary because if the Gypsies were able to get into the yard, they would take all the fruit from the trees and vegetables from the garden that was growing there. In fact, we had make sure that the car that we had driven from Budapest was hidden because of the fear that the Gypsies would disassemble the car and sell the parts if they could ever get their hands on it.

We learned from Josey that Anya had been taken to the hospital a few days before and was not doing so well because of extreme anemia.

The next morning Augi fixed breakfast for us before she went off to work at the hospital. Augi was in charge of the laundry. We walked over to the hospital to visit Anya and spoke with her doctor. We were visited by the chief of surgery at the hospital who invited us to his apartment for dinner that evening. The doctor and his wife had never met anyone from America before. I looked around in Anya's hospital room and saw an open box of feminine napkins sitting on the dresser. Ily asked her mother why the box of feminine napkins was sitting out like that. Ily had given that box of Kotex to her mother when she was in Atlanta visiting us the year before. Anya replied, "I could not remember what the purpose of the Kotex were, but they smelled so good that we have been putting them under our arms to help us smell better." It was then that I realized that I was in a country very different from the United States. The Romanians that I met had no concept of what we have here.

That evening we put on some fresh clothes and went to the chief surgeon's apartment for dinner. He and his wife confided in us in very low whispers, that they were also planning to leave Romania and travel to the West. The doctor asked me how I had gotten to Romania. He wanted to know by what means we had been able to come from the United States to Europe and I told him that I had taken a plane. He did not understand what I meant when I said "plane" and I had to explain that I flew on a jet airliner and arrived in Budapest. We had to explain that upon arrival we rented a car and drove from Budapest to Gorginni-hi. He then asked me a question that caused me to scratch my head. He asked, "How is it in America?"

I grew up in America; I had lived in several different cities both in the South and in New England.

There is a great diversity of culture, race, religion, wealth and poverty in the United States. There are liberals, conservatives, extremists of all sorts and middle-of-the-road everyday citizens from 50 different states in several regions throughout our country. There is a great diversity in America. While there were three main ethnic groups in Romania there are probably hundreds of different ethnic groups in the United States. The political divisions in the United States are much more profound and obvious than appeared to be the case in Romania. Regional differences between the North and the South are still very apparent in the United States. The divide between people living on the East Coast and West Coast (especially Californians; let alone the difference between Northern California and Southern California) are apparent even to casual observers of the American scene. I told the doctor that it was very difficult to answer his question as he had phrased it. I also told him that he could not possibly understand "how it is in America" by watching the television serial *Dallas*, even though it was the one television show that was allowed to be seen in Romania at that time. Life in Romania was very different from what I had experienced in the United States. The ability to speak up, complain, worship freely, succeed and fail are guarantees that each of us enjoy as citizens of the United States. Many of those rights could not be afforded to the citizens of Romania.

While we were driving from Oradea to Cluj it seemed like every mile there was a big billboard extolling the virtues of the Romanian dictator Ceausescu. There also billboards emphasizing the patriotism of Mrs. Ceausescu and reminding everyone that their life was so good because of leadership of their dictator. When I remember the propaganda that was evident in Romania in the late 1980s it brings to mind statements made by President Trump when he extols how great America has become while he has been president. In 1989, the people of Romania revolted, captured the dictator Ceausescu and hundreds of citizens lined up to shoot Ceausescu and his wife as they lay in the courtyard of the national Palace. It reminded me of a quote from Mark Twain who said, "Patriotism is supporting your country all the time, and supporting the government when it deserves it."

We remained in Gorginnihi for almost 2 weeks. We were continuously invited to lunch and dinner not only in Ily's hometown but also in the surrounding villages. Any time that anybody heard that an American was in town, we were invited to spend the day just so people could see what an American looked and acted like (I had gotten the idea that because of the propaganda being given to the Romanian people and because the only television show from America that they could watch was *Dallas,* that they probably thought that I should look and act like J R Ewing).

We brought lots of trinkets and clothing with us so that we could share with people that Ily knew and for those that would attend to Anya after we left. Ily sold all the sugar, coffee, and Pepsi that we had brought with us from Hungary. By the time that she had gotten through making all her trades, and selling our cloths, we had more Romanian currency than we could handle. At that time the Romanian currency was Ley. The official exchange rate at the border was eight Ley to a dollar. The unofficial exchange rate was more like 200 Ley to the dollar. By the time we were ready to leave we had accumulated enough crash so that Ily's mother could live very comfortably for the rest of her life.

One day Josey told us that he needed to go downtown to buy a pair of shoes. We went into the department store and went to the counter where shoes were sold. Josey told the clerk the size of shoes that he wanted. There was only one kind of shoe that you could buy, there was extremely little choice or styles of shoes offered. All the stores were owned by the government and all the means of production of shoes were also owned by the government. Whatever little trade went on between countries was limited to those countries in the communist bloc. And then because Romania was close to the Soviet Union there was even very little trade between Romania and other communist countries that were not within the Soviet bloc. The clerk told Josey that the size of shoe that he had asked for was sold out. It was at that point that I realized that the system in that communist country required that you grease the palm of the clerk in order to get your shoes. After we had sufficiently given the clerk a pack of Kent cigarettes she went into the back and just happened to find one pair of shoes the exact size that Josey had asked for.

Another day we were walking around in downtown Gorginnihi, and we saw a long line of people going into a store. Ily was interested to see what the line was for, and we got into the queue. After about a half an hour we were getting close to the front of the line when it occurred to us to ask what the purpose of our standing in that particular line was. It turned out that the people were in line to buy matches. Imagine that, standing in line to buy matches. Here we have matches just for the asking. There matches were a commodity that was necessary for everyday life. Their cooking stoves required a lit match to ignite the bottled gas that they use to cook with. Their heating system required a match to ignite the sawdust container that was soaked with kerosene that was the means of heating their homes. They did not have cigarette lighters. When I got to the front of the line the man behind me begged me to give him the supply of matches that I was about to buy. I did him one better, I happen to have a Bic lighter in my pocket that we had brought with us to give away. I pulled lighter out of my pocket and put it in his hand, he was so grateful that I think he wanted to kiss me.

In Romania men kiss each other on the lips as part of their greeting of each other. I was not in a position to allow that man to kiss me because I had known him but a few minutes and besides, in that country they only brush their teeth every so often. When we had first gotten to Gorginnihi, Josey greeted me with a lip smacker. I asked Ily to ask Josey if he ever brushed his teeth and he replied that he of course he brushed his teeth at least once a week.

Another day we were invited to Pesta Bacsi's (Uncle Pete's) house for lunch. Pesta is Hungarian for Pete, so we were invited to Uncle Pete's house. It turns out that it is good to have an Uncle Pete. As we were walking over to Pesta Bacsi's house we were stopped by one of Anya's friends who was curious to see that Ily was in town because she had heard that Ily was now living in America. Anya told this friend of hers that talk was cheap and that she could not stop and talk to her because we were late for lunch, and she was hungry. Unknown to me, but very well known to Anya we were only late by one day. Uncle Pete thought we were coming the day before but somehow time got mixed up and we arrived exactly one day late. Even though people had telephones they did not often call each other. Ily's mother did not have a phone.

We sat down for the meal, and we were served a shot of Tuika, which is a homemade plum brandy that is very potent. The Hungarians that we ate with traditionally served a shot of Tuika at the start of the meal and claim that it was good for invigorating your appetite. After the Tuika we were served chicken paprika. Hungarian cuisine is generally peasant fair and chicken paprika is a very traditional homegrown dish. While we were eating, I noticed that Uncle Pete and his wife were not eating, and I asked why. We were told that the chicken that we are eating had been their pet and now out of respect they would not eat their pet chicken. The next day we went to another of Ily's relatives for lunch, and again they served chicken paprika. Once again, these relatives did not eat while we ate, and again I asked why and again they said that the chicken was their pet. I then realized that there may not have been enough to go around so they were not eating the chicken paprika. Instead of admitting that they had not enough to go around they were claiming that the chicken was their pet so that they would ensure that their guests had enough.

After the chicken paprika we were served stuffed cabbage. There are as many variations of stuffed cabbage as there are families that serve it. My mother made stuffed cabbage when I was a child. Her recipe came from my Aunt Edith, my father's oldest sister. After enjoying the meal at Uncle Pete's, he brought out bottles of fig wine and insisted that we some take it home with us. We gave Uncle Pete some coffee and sugar and I think we even gave him a banana. Uncle Pete who at one time had worked as a manager of the local grocery store told us that he was very familiar with bananas and remembered back to the early 60s when they had received a shipment of bananas from Cuba. They hadn't seen any bananas since.

A few days later it was time for us to prepare to drive back to Budapest and return home. By then we were nearly out of gas, so we went to the local hotel in order to buy gas bonds. In Romania you just cannot drive up to a gas station and fill up. You have to present a gas bond which is the official method of exchange for buying gas. When we got to the clerk that was selling the gas bonds, we were informed that they did not have any. I panicked and had to rush down to the men's room. I could not see myself living in Romania for any more than the next few days. After delivering a few packs of Kent cigarettes to the gas bond clerk we were able to fill up the car and I was excited about leaving.

Before we left Josey and his friend Ariel decided to take me into the mountains to hunt for mushrooms. Hungarians prize mushrooms in their diet almost as much as hobbits. We each had a backpack in which we had a picnic lunch and a few bottles of beer. We found a spot, parked the car and ascended the very picturesque mountain in order to find wild mushrooms. After searching around for mushrooms for a little while (I did not know which ones were edible and which ones were not, but they did) I came upon a steaming pile of scat. I asked Josey what could have left that pile and he told me that it had been produced by a medva which is Hungarian for bear. Of all the causes of death that are available to humans it is my preference not to be eaten. I do not want to be eaten by a bear, a wolf, a shark or any other animal. I told Josey that it was time for us to go back to the car and have our lunch and he agreed. I felt better about hunting mushrooms after we got back to the car.

One last event that we participated in before we left Romania was the christening of Ily's niece, Caticha. The little girl was nearly three years old at the time that the christening event took place. Generally, christening takes place when the child is still considered an infant, but they decided to wait until we had made our way to Romania. Not only that but we were asked to be the godparents of the little girl. The Hungarians who live in Romania are mainly Roman Catholic while the Romanian part of the population is Eastern Orthodox. The other large segment of the population is made up of Gypsies, but it is uncertain what religion the Gypsies follow. In order for me to qualify as the Godfather for Caticha, I had to be able to recite the Lord 's Prayer in Hungarian. I practiced all day to be able to say that part of the Scripture in Hungarian and finally succeeded in doing a passable job. When we were getting ready to go to the church, they repeated the phrase that in essence said, "out from the house goes a sinner". When we returned home with the now christened child, we were greeted with the phrase that meant "in comes a Christian." Following the christening we had an all-night party. It was one of the few times that we were served meat. As it turned out meat was very scarce but on that day a bear had killed a cow, wink, wink. We enjoyed beef that evening along with lots of alcohol and other interesting portions of the ceremony.

Because Augi was the manager of the laundry at the hospital, she took our dirty clothes to be washed every day. After a few days I noticed that the underwear that I had brought with me that had been washed at the hospital laundry seemed to be full of starch. I had Ily ask Augi what she was putting in the wash to make my underwear so stiff. She replied that they had received a shipment of products from Germany that they believed was to be used in the laundry. I asked her to let me see the box in which the laundry product had been sent. While I do not read German very well it was clear to me that what they were putting into the laundry was an amalgamation that was intended to be used for making false teeth. When I told Augi that the product was not starch but was intended for making false teeth not only was she surprised but remarked that she wondered why the laundry had gotten so stiff.

When it was time to leave Romania, it was interesting to see children along the road waving to us as we drove by. There were not many cars on the road, and it was unusual to see a Western made car. At one point when we arrived at a friend's house, he was very interested in seeing the car that we were driving. In turn that man wanted to show us his Datchia, the only car made in Romania. When he presented his car he said, "Romanian Chevrolet."

Children in Romania often begged for chewing gum and I always seemed to have a supply of chewing gum in my pocket to pass out to the children. I often think of those children standing by the roadside, now many years ago and wonder what has become of them and how are the people and relatives that I met. I wonder how they are making their way in life now. I wonder whether the doctor that invited us to his apartment ever made it out of Romania and whether he is now somewhere in the West. And I wonder what Catchia's life has turned out to be.

After we crossed the border and returned to Hungary, I realized how much better life is here in the United States. Even in Hungry life was much better than it was in Romania. A few years later, the Romanian communist government was toppled; the dictator was killed along with his wife. The government palace in which Ceausescu lived was ransacked by a mob. There was much hope for a new beginning but whether that actually happened or not I cannot tell.

Betrayal

I stayed married to Ily for seven years. When we first got together, she had a job at Davison's department store that later became Macys. After she had been there for a short period of time, she was transferred to the Couture shop and would often bring home new dresses and outfits. Generally, she spent more money on her cloths than she made. After a while she became interested in pursuing a degree at Georgia State University studying graphic design. Ily had a real knack for putting together fashion designs and the print and photographic material that would be used in advertising the designs. We bought a high-end camera that she used in her studies. When her mother died, she returned to Romania for the funeral and was unable to continue her education that semester. She had been encouraged to become a fashion model and started to take the necessary steps in order to pursue that career. Eventually she appeared as a runway model during fashion week at the Fashion Mart in downtown Atlanta. She was also asked to be a part of the yearly Fashionata sponsored by Riches department store that also later became a part of Macy's.

Ily felt that she had achieved some success as a fashion model and that she should move on to more lucrative gigs. She was looking for other sources of money to allow her to achieve her dream of being a fashion model in New York City. After the communist government in Romania had toppled, news stories started to appear indicating that there were a vast number of orphans in Romania that were being neglected. There was an outpouring of interest on the part of many Americans to go to Romania and adopt these neglected children. Ily saw an opportunity to make some money assisting well-meaning Americans in obtaining these children by adoption. She was contacted by a family that lived in the Washington D C area and they struck a bargain as to what she would charge to assist them in finding and adopting a child in Romania. In March 1990 she and a member of the family that she had been contacted by traveled to Romania.

Before she left Atlanta it seemed like our life together was in very good shape. However, after she had been gone for two or three weeks it became more and more difficult to hear from her. She stopped calling me and I had no idea where she was. Ily succeeded in finding a child for the family that had hired her and the adoption procedure was underway. However, I did not know whether Ily was still in her hometown or exactly where she was at any given time. I had to continually check with the airlines to determine when she was scheduled to return to Atlanta.

The day finally arrived when I determined that Ily was on her way back to Atlanta. She was very surprised to see me at the airport when she got off the airplane. From that day forward Ily had very little to do with me. She did not want to sleep in the same bed with me any longer, did not want to touch me and certainly did not want me touching her. I was perplexed. Finally, one afternoon she told me that she wanted to go to dinner that evening, and we walked from our condo to downtown Decatur to eat at a restaurant that we often frequented. Ily suddenly told me that she was having pain and that she needed to go to the lady's room. She had a miscarriage, and it was all I could do to get her home that evening. She would not even allow me to drive her to the emergency room.

As it turned out the next day, we were supposed to drive to North Carolina to pick up my children who had been staying with my parents. Ily of course could not go but she insisted that I go without her. While I was driving, I was searching around in the car and found an audiotape that Ily had left in the glove compartment. I put the tape in the tape player and was heartbroken when I heard her and her astrologist plan on how to stick me with all of Ily's bills while she took off to New York. I was deeply depressed when I also heard her talking about the man that she had met in Romania and how she planned to return to see him in a few weeks.

When I got to my parents' home to pick up my children, I did not know what to do. Finally, I decided to call Ily and to confront her with the information that I had gained from listening to the audio tape. At first, she denied everything but when I told her that I had the tape and heard her words she hung up on me. A few minutes later she called back to tell me that it was true and that she planned on leaving me, returning to Germany to be with her new lover. Needless to say, I was heartsick, confused, dazed and felt betrayed. In church that Sunday after learning about Ily's intentions I decided that I could forgive her. The only condition that I felt to be appropriate was that she should not go forward with her plan on going back to Germany to see this new man. I told her that if she got on the airplane to go back to Germany that she should not return to me.

When I finally returned to Atlanta, I realize that Ily had taken out several credit cards in my name and had maxed out those cards. One afternoon she told me that she was going to leave the next day and that she wanted me to agree to give her $50,000 and to pay off all of her debts. I told her that there was still a chance that we could reconcile but that if she got on the airplane and went back to Germany that I could not go forward with our marriage. The next day she took a cab to the airport and went back to Germany. She left me with her cat, her debt, and broken heart. Not only that, but she also refused to pay cat support. When Thanksgiving came around that fall, I was miserable. I did not want to talk to anybody I did not want to eat; I wanted to crawl under the bed and die.

Teaching Sunday School

I started teaching Sunday school in 1977 or 1978. At first, I was asked to teach children but eventually was asked to take over teaching the oldest ladies Sunday school class at church. I felt called to teach the Bible and felt as if the ladies that were in my class benefited from having a regular Sunday school teacher even though I was very much younger than they. Within a few years of teaching in the Sunday school class I was asked to become the superintendent of the Sunday schools at the church. When my marriage to Phyllis ended and I became involved with Ily we began to attend the Druid Hills Baptist Church.

Shortly after joining Druid Hills Baptist, I was asked to teach a younger adult Sunday school class. Ily attended regularly with me and decided that she wanted to become baptized. She had grown up as a Roman Catholic but made a profession of faith and promised to follow Jesus. After a few years at Druid Hills, she wanted to change churches and we started to attend the First Baptist Church of Decatur. Within a few months after starting to attend First Baptist I was again asked to teach an adult Bible class. When Ily left me and moved to New York I continued to teach Sunday school. I am sure that my class was aware of my circumstances. But to my great disappointment, people that I had known for several years turned their backs on me and I felt as if no one cared. Eventually that led me to a time in which I stopped going to church and more importantly withdrew into myself.

While I was trying the Brown Realty cases I met Mike Froman. We became close friends and eventually he came to work in my office. Mike had been working on a case also involving the Brown Realty Company and was interested in how I was approaching the trial. This is the same Mike Froman that is discussed in the novel *Praying for Sheet Rock* written by Melissa Fay Green that discusses Mike's involvement in the legal services community in South Georgia. Mike is a Graduate of the Harvard School of Law, and when we met, he was a sole practitioner in Decatur.

Trial in Rome

While the Brown Realty cases were going on and after Mike had joined me at Sakas & Horne, I got Mike to assist me in a trial in Rome Georgia. In that matter I represented a contractor who had gotten a job in Somerville, Georgia doing the concrete work on the prison that was under construction just out of Summerville. After my client had successfully bid on the concrete work, one of her trusted employees decided to form his own company and re-negotiate the concrete work on the prison with the general contractor. My client's employee's name was Ed and he had had years of experience in the building industry. The general contractor was a regional construction firm that was looking to cut their costs and therefore agreed to breach their contract with my client and allow Ed and his newly formed company to complete the work at the prison. Under Georgia law an employee owes a duty of loyalty to his employer and a breach of that duty is tantamount to a fraud. Additionally, if an interested person knew of the breach of the fiduciary duty of the employee and did an act in furtherance of the breach that person became a conspirator in the illegal act.

In the particular case that we were undertaking in Rome on behalf of my client it was clear that Ed while he was an employee formed a new business, took the business opportunity that my client had contracted for, conspired with the general contractor and damaged my client. I filed suit for breach of fiduciary duty, fraud, breach of contract, and conspiracy to commit fraud against the former employee, his new business and the general contractor. The case was to be tried in late winter in Rome in the Superior Court of Floyd County. Rome is about 70 miles northwest of Atlanta and while we could have driven back and forth on a daily basis, we chose to get a hotel room and stay in Rome during the trial.

In outlying counties, such as Floyd County, the list of potential jurors is often published a few days prior to the actual start of the trial. That is generally not the case in the urban counties around Atlanta. In the case that I was getting ready to try I was able to obtain the jury list and enlisted the aid of a local attorney to assist me in going over the jury list to determine the background of potential jurors. On Sunday afternoon prior to the trial of the case I met with an older attorney in Rome who gave me some valuable insight into potential jurors. Later that evening, I contacted another member of the Georgia Trial Lawyers Association and asked if he had any insight concerning potential jurors. It turned out that he was also going to be trying a case the next day in Floyd Superior court and he was going over the list of potential jurors that evening. I met him at his office around 8 PM. As we were going over the list, he pointed out that there was a woman on the jury pool who was having an affair with my opposing counsel. Had I not gone over the jury list with that local attorney I would have had no idea about that potential juror. As it turned out that particular lady was on the panel of potential jurors that was assigned to my case. Based on the information that I had been given I was able to strike her off the jury. Needless to say, I dodged a bullet on that one.

After jury selection the trial started, and everything seemed to be going fairly well for my side. My client was nervous but satisfied with the way the evidence was being presented. One of the issues in the case was whether a profit could actually be made by the way the contract for the concrete was bid. The defense produced an accountant who was going to testify that there was no profit to be made in that particular contract. That accountant had not been provided to us for discovery and I asked the court to allow us to examine documents related to the accountant's opinions after the recess for the day. The judge ordered that the opposing attorney allow us to come to his office that evening to examine the relevant documents. I asked Mike if he would go to the other lawyer's office and spend a few hours examining the relevant documents while I was preparing for the next day of testimony. Later that evening, Mike and I met, and he was very excited. He had uncovered a letter in the other lawyer's files indicating that the accountant had agreed to a change his testimony for additional compensation. In other words the accountant was willing to cook his books for money.

When the trial resumed the next morning, the accountant was still under cross-examination, and I began to ask him questions concerning whether or not he had changed his testimony and he stated under oath that he would never changes testimony and that what he had stated under oath under direct examination was the truth. At that point I produce the letter that Mike had found in the opposing lawyer's files. My heart was racing, the accountant's face became bright red, and he coughed and sputtered almost uncontrollably. He agreed that he had changed his testimony based on additional compensation and that he had lied under oath. The case eventually went to the jury and the jury returned a substantial verdict in my client's favor.

Mike Froman

After a few years of practicing law with Mike, he decided that he wanted to become a computer programmer and decided that he would take programming courses at Georgia State University. One of the classes that he had to take was a computer language called C++. After he had been in the class for a week or so the professor pulled Mike aside and told him that he had to withdraw from the class. The professor told Mike that because he did not have calculus on his transcript, which was a prerequisite for the C++ class, that he could not continue. Evidently, a few exams had already taken place and Mike told the professor that he was making the highest grade in the class and that he should be allowed to continue. The professor insisted that Mike withdraw. The professor told Mike that if he wanted to continue in the class that he had to go and discuss the matter with the head of the math department. Mike met with the head of the math department and again Mike was told that he could not continue in the C++ course because he did not have calculus on his transcript. Mike informed the professor that he had a degree in mathematics from the University of Minnesota, that he had a master's in mathematics from MIT and had everything but a final dissertation for his PhD in mathematics from MIT. The head of the math department looked at Mike and said, "Would you like to teach calculus here at Georgia State? We are always looking for calculus professors." Mike completed the C++ class and of course made the highest grade.

Unfortunately, Harold Horne decided that it was time for our relationship to come to an end. Mike and I moved to a new office location and Harold got an office in an office suite situation a few buildings over from where Mike and I were located. One afternoon I got a call from one of the lawyers that knew both Harold and me asking if I had heard from Harold recently. No one at Harold's new office had heard from him in for several days and people were beginning to get worried. Harold suffered from juvenile onset diabetes and as the years had gone by Harold's condition had become more brittle. I recall one day I came to the office and Harold was lying in the floor, frothing at the mouth. Another time I found Harold riding up and down on the elevator oblivious to what was going on around him. When those things happened, I would take Harold to the closest restaurant and make him eat. Once he had eaten, he was able to come back to normal.

When nobody could find Harold, Mike, me and one of the secretaries in the office drove to Harold's condo. When we got there his car was in the driveway but when I knocked on the door there was no answer. After a few minutes I could smell the worst smell that I have ever encountered, the smell of a decaying body. I called the police, they entered Harold's condo and found him dead in his bedroom. A half-eaten cake and an empty bottle of wine indicated that he had decided to give up and ingest those things that he probably knew would wind up killing him. The police informed his family and Mike and I drove to Americus for his funeral.

Fleet Finance

The Brown Realty cases that I had tried in 1988 brought media attention to me. The trial had been covered in the Atlanta Journal-Constitution and there were news reports on television. I started to get calls from others who had had bad experiences with mortgage companies concerning home repair loans. I started to investigate these allegations and was again contacted by Bill Brennan at the Atlanta Legal Aid Society concerning this new series of cases. We started to see what we called the "Tin Man" scenario.

Typically, a siding or a roofing company would scout low-income neighborhoods and find generally older individuals living in houses that needed repairs. Actually, there was a movie, *The Tin Man*, that came out around that time starring Danny DeVito as an unscrupulous door to door salesman preying on uninformed consumers. In Atlanta we found that home repair companies were targeting black neighborhoods. The "tin man" would get the homeowner to enter into a contract for home repairs. The home repair work was financed by the homeowner by signing a second mortgage on their home. The "tin man" would then sell the paper (promissory note and second deed to secure debt) to a finance company. Later, we identified seven finance companies willing to take these loans and to pay the "tin man" prior to performing the work. We began to call the tin man financing companies "The Seven Dwarves."

Generally, the work that was being performed by the tin man companies was substandard and these homeowners started showing up at my office telling the same stories. Bill Brennan, at the Atlanta

126

Legal Aid Society Home Defense Fund was also seeing his share of these kinds of cases. We also learned that the seven finance companies that were buying the "tin man's" paper (that is when we started calling the seven finance companies the "seven dwarfs") were in turn selling the paper to Fleet Finance Company. Fleet Finance was a subsidiary of Fleet Bank that had its headquarters in Boston. I started getting inquiries from national newspapers concerning what was going on in the Atlanta housing market and especially with Fleet Finance. We had a breakthrough in our investigation when one of the principles of one of the "seven dwarves" called me and laid out for me the way that the "Tin Man" scheme worked.

The Atlanta Legal Aid Society asked me to get involved with them in filing a complaint naming the seven dwarves and Fleet Finance as defendants. We decided to file the case in the United States Federal Court in Atlanta and seek class-action representation for our clients. The basis for the Legal Aid case was fraud and usury. I worked with a group of lawyers and my job was to deal with the class-action allegations. Eventually we sought certification of the case as a class-action, but no action was taken by the District Court.

Almost simultaneously with the filing of the Legal Aid case in federal court, I was also contacted by Roy Barnes, a lawyer in Marietta and a state legislator about joining forces with his group to also go after Fleet. Roy Barnes later became governor of Georgia. Another lawyer in Roy's office, Howard Goldbloom, who did mostly bankruptcy cases, also became involved in the planning and execution of the litigation against Fleet. We settled on Lily May Star as the class representative and filed our complaint in the Superior Court of Cobb County. Roy Barnes enjoyed a very good reputation in Cobb County and his political connections did not hurt. The case in Cobb Superior Court was assigned to Judge Grant Brantley. Judge Brantley after considering our petition for class certification, certified our case as a class-action.

Judge Brantley had broken party barriers when he became a Superior Court judge. He was the first Republican to be elected as a Superior Court judge in Cobb County. Shortly after our case was certified as a class-action, judge Brantley retired from the bench because he was under consideration for a federal appointment by the president, who at that time was George H. W. Bush. Before Judge Brantley could be appointed to the federal bench, Bill Clinton was elected as president and Judge Brantley withdrew from consideration for the federal bench. Judge Brantley was replaced on the Cobb Superior Court by Judge Mary Staley who would prove to be a very capable and fair jurist.

The Legal Aid Society case that was being pursued in federal court was not proceeding efficiently. The Federal judge denied our petition for class certification, and we were having a hard time fending off motions for summary judgment. The cause of action that was being pursued in federal court was based on violations of the truth in lending laws, and fraud. On the other hand, the case that I was pursuing in Cobb County required a total change of direction from the theories that we were pursuing in federal court. I started to study the provisions of the federal RICO law and its effects on the law of Georgia. I started to read about how in the 1930s there was a concerted effort by the federal government to deal with loan sharks. The loansharking laws had been made predicate acts under the federal RICO statute. There were two prongs to the loansharking laws: extortionate extension of credit, and extortionate collection of credit. As discussed earlier, there is a Georgia state RICO act that in some respects is similar to the federal RICO act, however there are significant differences. Perhaps the main difference is that federal law requires the proof that the organization be characterized as a criminal enterprise. Under Georgia law it is sufficient that anyone that commits two or more predicate acts can be liable under the state version of RICO.

Extortion is a very interesting concept. Under Georgia law there is no civil cause of action for extortion, but the crime of extortion had also been made a part of the predicate acts under the Georgia RICO statute. Extortion can be defined as causing someone to take an action based upon a threat of either physical harm or making a threat that would impact the victim's property. The federal law contemplated extortionate loans in which the loan shark would loan money at very high rates of interest (in violation of the usury laws of the state in which the loan was made) or collecting such loans by means of threats. Typically, one would think about the character portrayed by Sylvester Stallone in the first Rocky movie in which the character, Rocky Balboa, is tasked with collecting money for the mob boss by breaking bones.

The law of usury in Georgia is not very clear. When we started to try to figure out the best cause of action to use in the Fleet cases, we looked carefully at what could be considered a usurious loan. Under Georgia law it is legal to loan money at 5% interest per month. A 60% interest rate per year is not illegal in Georgia. The question often is asked, "How does one determine a true interest rate when fees for making the loan are also paid by the debtor and financed over the term of the loan?" It was our job to convince the court that Fleet was engaging in extortion and our investigation led us in several different directions. First, we learned that Fleet aggressively collected its loans by calling its debtors on a monthly basis and threatening foreclosure on their properties and ruining their credit if they did not make immediate payment.

Later, during the discovery phase of the litigation we were able to discover that Fleet calculated interest on its loans on a daily basis. Usually, interest is calculated on a monthly basis. Often the promissory note states that the interest rate on the loan is x% on any unpaid balance. Fleet stated in a deposition that they had a method called a CP2 in which they calculated interest from the date of the last payment until the date of the next payment and if the amount paid did not fully pay all the interest that accrued that they would set up an account within each particular loan that accrued interest outside of the payment schedule that its creditors believed would satisfy the outstanding portion of the loan. In other words, on a loan that had an interest rate of 12% or 14% (the typical interest rate charged on these "tin man" loans) and the payment on the loan was represented to be $450, if the payment was not received on the exact due date, there was an extra day or two of interest charged to the loan and that amount was accounted for separately. Under Fleets method of calculating interest on these loans the consumer never knew exactly how much was owed at any given time and Fleet was able to charge the consumer in such a way that it made it extremely difficult to pay off the loan. Among the lawyers working on the Fleet case, we began to believe that Fleets loans were like checking into "The Hotel California" because you could check out, but you never could leave.

While we were pursuing our causes of action in federal court and in Cobb Superior, we became aware that a competing class-action had also been filed in Augusta. The cause of action in Augusta also sought class certification and was based primarily on claims of usury. Usury is a legal principle that puts a legal limit on the amount of interest that can be charged on outstanding loans. The Truth in Lending laws of the United States requires that lenders in certain circumstances disclose the interest rates that are being charged to consumers. The various states have their own particular laws on the amount of interest that can be charged on an outstanding loan. Under Georgia law the maximum that can be charged is 5% per month or a total of 60% per year on outstanding loans.

The group of lawyers in Atlanta began to have regular meetings with the lawyers in Augusta. The lawyers in Augusta had educated their judges on the issue of class certification, and they were able to obtain class certification on a regular basis on cases that they filed in Richmond County. On a few occasions the lawyers from Augusta attended depositions that I had scheduled in Atlanta. Roy Barnes was instrumental in dealing with the lawyers in Augusta and based on the results of several meetings the Augusta lawyers backed off from challenging our right to pursue our class-action. That was essentially true because the cause of action that we were pursuing was different from the cause of action that they were pursuing.

After fending off motions for summary judgment filed by Fleet, settlement discussions were initiated. Once a class-action is certified by the court the defense strategy often shifts from a vigorous defense of the particular claims made in the complaint to one of washing all the dirty laundry (any cause of action that might be brought against the defendant by the class) that they can possibly cram into the litigation. That means that in this case Fleet wanted to include as many claims as possible that could be made against it so that the preclusive effect (preclusion in this instance means an end to all potential causes of action that plaintiffs could make against Fleet so as to prevent any further claims) would affect the greatest number of potential claimants.

Settlement discussions went on for several months with Roy Barnes taking the lead in negotiating. I was not in favor of settling at that point in the litigation and strongly believed that because of the publicity that we were receiving that it would be more rewarding to try the case to a jury. During the prosecution of the case the 60 Minutes television show became interested in the litigation and set up an interview with us. Again, Roy Barnes took the lead and was interviewed on camera for one of the weekly segments on that television program. When asked about the type of cause of action that we were pursuing, Roy in his usual down-home manner told the interviewer, "I don't know what y- all call that up in New York but down here in Georgia, we call it cheatin' and stealin'."

Constance Heard came to work in my office sometime in 1993 or 1994. She had just graduated from Georgia State University law school. I had met her when she called to ask if I would represent her family in a real estate dispute that was going on in Athens, Georgia. Interestingly, hearings in that particular case would start at 6 in the evening. Constance would pick me up and we would ride to Athens in her car. One night on the way home from a particularly late hearing she asked me to come into her house for a late evening snack. The snack that she contemplated was a physical relationship. When she came to work in my office, I asked her to assist me in doing research at Emory Law School. At that time we still used books instead of online libraries. Constance would also attend meetings with me at Roy Barnes office to discuss the work that needed to be accomplished.

One of the attorneys in Roy's office was assigned certain responsibilities regarding discovery and response to Fleet's motion to compel discovery. At the last minute that attorney bailed out and I was left holding the proverbial bag. I had to take a few lumps for the team at that time.

While all of this was going on, Ali, my daughter was in high school. Ali was a member of the high school chorus and had a solo part in the holiday music presentation of her choir. I recall one evening after having met at Roy Barnes office to discuss the Fleet case that I hurried down to Riverdale to hear Ali sing. She had a beautiful voice, and her performance was very dear to me.

During that time, we also had several more meetings with the attorneys in Augusta in order to resolve the competing elements of the two class actions that had now been certified, the class-action that we filed in the Superior Court of Cobb County and the class-action that they had filed in the Superior Court of Richmond County. The lawyers in Augusta would call me from time to time to tell me that the settlement that we had proposed with Fleet was inadequate to cover all the claims that were being asserted. While the legal wrangling was going on between the lawyers in Augusta and us, a new ruling from the Supreme Court of Georgia made it clear that a claim based on usury was not going to go very far. That left our claim based on loansharking to be the most viable claim.

Roy handled almost all the negotiations and reported to us when specific offers were made. A settlement proposal was finally made in which Fleet offered to settle our case for a total of $5 million. I did not believe that that amount was sufficient to make adequate distributions to the potential members of the class. I met Roy for breakfast in downtown Atlanta and explained my misgivings. Prior to that meeting Roy had always told me how appreciative he was of the work that I was doing and especially the brief writing that I was submitting to the court. At our breakfast meeting he began to tell me how little work I had performed in this case and that I did not deserve an equal share of the legal fees that were being generated. Roy's criticism of my work was unfair. I had done the bulk of the legal work in that case, had written all the briefs, complaints, had taken all the depositions and had put the case in a position to succeed. Howard Goldbloom had worked hard in keeping the clients together and obtaining documentation and evidence in support of our case. The other lawyers involved did not do too much. I told Roy that I was a team player and that I would not make any waves concerning the acceptance of the proposed settlement even though I had big reservations concerning the adequacy of the amounts involved. The case settled I received a substantial fee, I paid Constance for her help, and we moved on.

Working with Yehuda

In 1995 I started sharing space in Yehuda Smolar's office. Yehuda by that time had hired Grant Brantley the former Superior Court Judge who had certified the Fleet case for class-action status. Yehuda had a case in federal court concerning the death of a young lady in an automobile collision. Yehuda had filed the case in Cobb County but the insurance company that had excess coverage filed a declaratory judgment action in federal court in order to determine whether the insurance policy had lapsed prior to the automobile accident that had killed this young lady. A declaratory judgment action is a proceeding in which the plaintiff in the case alleges that they need a decision by the court concerning a legal issue or a fact issue that may be determinative of the case prior to litigating liability. In other words, in this particular case, the insurance company that was ensuring the automobile in which Yehuda's client was a passenger, contended that the policyholder (owner of the car) had allowed the umbrella policy (an insurance policy that provided additional protection to the policyholder) to lapse by failing to pay the premium on the policy.

Originally my friend Seton Purdum had been hired by Yehuda to come up with a defense. The underlying insurance policy that provided liability coverage was not adequate to fully compensate our clients for the death of their daughter. The umbrella policy provided an additional one million dollars in coverage and therefore it was necessary to have that policy in effect so as to fully compensate our clients. When a declaratory judgment action is filed the liability case is stayed (held in abeyance) until the court decides the rights of the insurance company.

As it turned out the premium for the umbrella coverage was due very close to the time that the client's daughter had been killed in the accident that was the basis of the underlying cause of action. The facts indicated that the insurance company had failed to send a proper notice of cancellation of the umbrella policy and therefore a legal issue of whether the umbrella policy was still in effect on the date of the accident became the issue for trial in the declaratory judgment action.

Seton who at one time had been my law clerk when I was still at Jesse, Ritchie & Duncan grew up in Decatur, Georgia. His father had been a well-known attorney in Decatur and his cousin, Wayne Purdum later became the chief judge of the State Court of DeKalb County. Seton had laid out the facts in a motion for summary judgment but for some reason the Federal Court had not made a decision. The case had been assigned to Judge Horace Ward. Judge Ward when he was a much younger man tried to integrate the University of Georgia law school but was prevented from enrolling there. Judge Ward graduated from Michigan State and became a judge, first In the State Court of Fulton County, then in the Superior Court and finally he ascended to the United States District Court. I had tried a case before Judge Ward when he was in the State Court and had had a previous case before him In the Federal Court.

The case got ready for trial and by that time Seton was no longer in the case and Yehuda asked me to represent one of the parties. Yehuda and Grant Brantley represented the parents of the young lady who had been killed and I represented the driver of the automobile in which the young lady was a passenger. The case boiled down to one legal issue. Judge Ward kept putting off a decision concerning the issue of whether the notice sent by the insurance company to the policyholder was adequate to cause the policy to lapse.

At the end of a typical trial, lawyers submit to the court what is known as jury charges which are statements of law that the court must read to the jury and to which the jury must apply the facts in order to come to a verdict. It was at that point in the trial that I was able to force judge Ward to make a decision as to whether he would read the law that applied to the particular facts that the notice sent by the insurance company was not adequate. When he finally decided that he had to give that jury charge it was clear that he then had to grant a directed verdict in our favor, which he did. Grant Brantley was very impressed with how I put the judge in a situation in which he had to finally make a decision as to the applicable law. Shortly after we won the Declaratory Judgment Action, Yehuda was able to reach a settlement that gave adequate compensation to the parents of the young lady who was killed in the accident.

There was always a problem between Yehuda and those that worked with him on cases. Yehuda would make a promise to pay someone like me a reasonable amount of money to assist him in his cases but when it came time to divvy up the money Yehuda always forgot what he had previously promised, and it was very difficult to pry the money loose after the money went into his account. That became a reoccurring problem over the years that I worked with Yehuda on his cases.

After the declaratory judgment action was resolved another very interesting case showed up in the office. A company, Open MRI, had a sales technique in which they offered kickbacks to doctors who referred patients to Open MRI to have studies of their spines and other bodily parts. Open MRI was actually a group of offices in and around Atlanta. They were in the process of going public and a major stock brokerage company was going to serve as their underwriter in their public offering. When we determined that Open MRI was offering kickbacks, we went to work to determine whether there was any law that would prohibit that method of marketing their services. We determined that under the Federal Medicare act there was a clear prohibition of that method of marketing. Additionally, under Georgia law there was both an anti-kickback statute and a statute that prohibited doctors from sharing fees.

Yehuda asked me to draw up a complaint seeking class certification for the plaintiff/patients of doctors who had been referred to Open MRI. Additionally, I was tasked with describing a defendant class of doctors who had violated the anti-kickback laws. I quickly drafted such a complaint, and we filed that complaint in the State Court of Fulton County. As you would expect there was major legal talent lined up against us. Lin Wood who went to work with Jim Jesse right after the breakup of Jesse Ritchie & Duncan and who had represented the parents of Jon Benet Ramsey after that poor little girl had been found murdered was to act as lead counsel for Open MRI. In addition to Lynn Wood who at that time was a sole practitioner, was the firm of Powell Goldstein Fraser & Murphy, a mega firm that had several hundred attorneys. In addition to drawing up the complaint I also had the responsibility of finding an appropriate class representative. I finally settled on a former client of mine by the name of Steve Blanton who had been involved in an automobile accident, was being treated by a group of orthopedic doctors in

Fayetteville, Georgia and who had been sent by them to one of the Open MRI offices.

I had represented Steve and his wife in a case against Citizens and Southern National Bank in a fraud and RICO scheme several years before. Steve had a colorful background and had spent some time at state expense. Steve and wife Donna lived in Senoia, Georgia which is in the extreme south of Metropolitan Atlanta. Steve worked for a company that collected garbage. He drove one of those trucks that picked up dumpsters and emptied them into the big container on the back of the truck. While Steve was driving in Newnan, Georgia the truck he was driving was broadsided by an older lady and Steve was injured to the extent that he could not continue to work. While Steve was not an ideal class representative, I had known him for several years and knew that I could count on him to work with me on the case against Open MRI.

The case got started, some discovery took place, and the attorneys for Open MRI filed a series of motions to have the case dismissed. We hired my old friend Susan Garrett to help with the research and writing. The main question in the case was whether the Georgia statute that prohibited doctors from sharing fees provided a civil cause of action that could be used in order to recover damages. Susan did a very good job in preparing our brief in response to Open MRI's Motion to Dismiss and we convinced the court to allow us to go forward with the litigation. Open MRI then filed a motion for summary judgment, and we were able to convince the court to deny their motion. Shortly thereafter settlement negotiations began in earnest. The court had not as of that time ruled upon our motion to certify the case as a class-action. Had the court certified the case, settlement discussions would have had to include perhaps as many as 3000 patients who had been referred to Open MRI and who had been caught up in the kickback scheme.

I worked fairly closely with Yehuda in negotiating the terms of the settlement and in working with the Georgia State Bar in order to get an opinion that we could dismiss the class action component of the case. There is some authority especially under the Manual for Complex Litigation in the federal system that indicates that once a case is filed as a class-action that it cannot be dismissed until the court rules on whether the case shall proceed as a class-action or not. Because our court had not considered class-action status and that issue was still outstanding; we felt it necessary to go to the Georgia State Bar and ask for a private ruling as to whether we could dismiss the class component without getting in trouble. After we were able to get a ruling from the State Bar, we were able to reach a settlement that was confidential. Some states do not allow confidentiality in the amount of settlements in cases like the ones that we had brought against Open MRI. Georgia is one of the few states that still allow defendants to insist on confidentiality concerning the terms of settlement.

Again, I had written the complaint, did all the research regarding the applicable statutes, and except for the assistance of Susan Garrett, wrote all the briefs. I argued all the motions before the court and actively participated in the settlement negotiations. Again, Yehuda insisted upon handling the checks and I had to agree to lend money to Yehuda in order to get my portion of the fees. Yehuda has never repaid the loan that I made him.

While the Open MRI case was wrapping up, we started getting clients who were students at Life Chiropractic College in Marietta, and again Yehuda called on me to quickly draft a complaint for class-action on behalf of Life Chiropractic students because Life had lost its accreditation.

There are generally two schools of thought among those that are practicing chiropractors. One school of thought is referred to as straight chiropractic and the other school of thought was called mixed chiropractic. Straight chiropractors believe that all elements of the body can be treated by manipulation of the spine.

Shortly after the Open MRI case settled, I decided it was time to leave Yehuda's office and seek another office from which to continue my practice. By then I was married to Elaine, and we had moved into what I consider to be a starter castle in unincorporated DeKalb County. I shared an office in Decatur with a group of lawyers that included Richard Green, Randall Mangum, Mary White and Susan Ellis. Richard had been a judge in the Recorders Court, Randall was in the state legislature, Mary and her husband had political influence and Susan was married to Judge Purdum.

Shortly after I moved into that office, I had to prepare for trial in a medical malpractice case. I represented an old friend who I had played softball with in the early 80s. Danny Maloney was a respiratory therapist at Henry County hospital. One evening when he was responding to a life flight at the helicopter pad, he slipped while running up an embankment and injured his back. We were able to settle his Worker's Comp. case, but he was further injured when his neurosurgeon misplaced a surgical screw causing the tip of the screw to be inserted into his spinal cord at the L-4-5 level. The damage to Danny's spinal cord was permanent and caused a loss of feeling in his left leg and caused pain from his low back all the way down to his foot. Danny was required to take a drug, Neurontin, which also had the side effect of making Danny impotent.

I filed Danny's case in the State Court of Fulton County; I hired an expert who was a practicing neurosurgeon from Providence Rhode Island. The defense hired an expert that practiced out of the Massachusetts Medical Center in Boston. During discovery one of the doctors that practiced along with the defendant admitted in his deposition that the placement of the pedicle screw in question in this case amounted to negligence. Based on that testimony I felt that we had a very good shot at prevailing at trial, even though convincing a jury that a doctor has committed medical malpractice is a very hard area of persuasion.

Prior to trial I asked Susan Garrett to assist me during the trial. When we finally got to the point of picking the jury and I conducted the voir dire. Voir dire is the portion of the trial in which the attorney is able to ask potential jurors questions concerning whether they have any preconceived notions that might prevent them from having an open mind and considering all the evidence. I specifically asked potential jurors whether there was any potential juror that for any reason could not render a verdict against a doctor particularly in a case in which the doctor had caused injury to his patient. Each of the potential jurors responded that they could render such a verdict. We tried the case for a week in April 2003. During the trial when I expected to call the doctor from the defendant's office who had testified that in his opinion, his partner had committed malpractice, counsel on the other side of the case were able to prevent that doctor's from testifying. The opposing attorney contended that the doctor's wife had an emergency and therefore he could not come to court. The judge that was handling the case allowed the defense to proceed without requiring that doctor to testify. I believed that I had been sandbagged by the defense lawyers.

Late in the day on Good Friday, the jury received the final instructions from the court. The jury deliberated for about five hours and returned a defense verdict. The next day I received a call from the woman who had been selected as the jury foreperson who told me that I needed to appeal the verdict because two female jurors had caused the jury to return a defense verdict. The juror on the other end of the phone told me that at the first vote after the case went to the jury that 10 of the jurors had voted for a plaintiff's verdict but these two women told the rest of the jurors that they would never agree to a verdict against a doctor despite what they had stated in voir dire. Needless to say I was heartbroken. I had sunk between $50,000 and $60,000 of my own money into preparation of the case and getting expert testimony. I had been lied to by potential jurors and my friend Danny was not going to be able to recover for his injuries.

Health Issues

Within a month or two I began to experience some health issues of my own. One day while I was working out at the health club, my heart started racing and when I walked into the dressing room to change clothes, I found myself lying on the floor having passed out. While I was lying on the floor one of the men in the dressing room told me that he was a doctor and that I should immediately go to the hospital. My heart had been racing but I felt that it was caused by the fact that I had just gone through an extremely long workout. I did not go to the hospital, and I felt better after I had rested for a short time. A week or so later Elaine and I went on a cruise through the Panama Canal. While we were on the cruise, I experienced my heart racing and I had to sit and rest for a few minutes for my heart to calm down.

When we finally got back to Atlanta, I had to go to court in Fulton County. I decided to take MARTA to the court and returned to Decatur also on MARTA. On my way back to the office I became extremely thirsty and stopped off at the Chick-fil-A that was on the way from the MARTA station to my office. After I left the Chick-fil-A my heart started racing and I became very faint. I had to lean against a telephone pole to prevent myself from falling into the street. After I recovered a little, I finally made it to my office. When I walked in the front door the receptionist, Ann Donnon, looked at me and said that I needed to go immediately to the emergency room. As I stated earlier that was a time that dramatically changed my life. It was not long after that that I decided that I had to end my marriage to Elaine.

After I had experienced the ventricular tachy-cardia (a/k/a v-tach) and had the defibrillator placed in my chest, I received a call from another attorney in Decatur who had heard that I had experience in handling class-action litigation. Joe Weeks was a young lawyer who practiced with an old friend of mine, Tom McNally. I had played softball with Tom in my earlier days and Tom's partner Steve Edwards had been a member of my Sunday school class when I taught at First Baptist Decatur. Both Tom and Steve were well respected members of the local bar. Joe was much younger. He contacted me concerning a potential class-action involving a heating and air-conditioning company that was also well recognized in the community.

Our client had hired the HVAC Company because her air-conditioner had gone out. The HVAC Company installed a new system but there were problems with the installation. Joe had discovered that the company had not gotten a building permit from the county and therefore in our opinion the installation of the new system violated county ordinances. In that situation the question became whether a violation of the county ordinance for failure to obtain a building permit allowed for a civil remedy against the HVAC Company. My experience with the Open MRI case told me that it was possible to obtain a civil verdict for violation of the county ordinance. It was our intent to file the cause of action in DeKalb County because we thought that would be a more favorable jurisdiction. Unfortunately, the HVAC Company did not have an office in DeKalb County and therefore we had to file the cause of action in Clayton County that in our opinion was a very less favorable jurisdiction.

Before the judge in Clayton County, we were unable to convince the court that a violation of county ordinances amounted to a civil cause of action and the Superior Court judge refused to consider our motion for class certification. We wound up settling the case and we were able to receive a settlement amount that our client and her attorneys were able to live with. After that case settled Joe and Tom asked if I would like to join them in their office and because it was a substantially better location than where I was at the time I accepted.

Lynn

One of my old clients, Shirley Lester, who had been one of the victims of the Brown Realty foreclosure fraud scheme, asked me to represent her granddaughter who had written a bad check. Lynn was a young unmarried woman who had a young daughter. Lynn was unemployed, lived in an apartment complex near Union City. She had written a bad check to Union City for the payment of her water bill. Shirley and Lynn came to my office, and I agreed to try to help Lynn with her legal problem. I attended court on her behalf in the recorders Court in Union City. I was able to work out an agreement with the solicitor that was favorable to Lynn. She could not pay the fee that I had quoted to her, but she did invite me to her apartment for dinner a few days later. When I arrived at her apartment, she greeted me at the door wrapped in a bath towel and invited me into her bathroom while she completed her bath. I should have known better than to get involved, but by that time I had been separated from Elaine for several months and was lonely.

Lynn claimed to be a Pentecostal Christian who was able to prophesy concerning future events. She was ambitious but had been limited in her ability to find work. Her daughter, Jasmine, limited Lynn's ability to get out and meet people and to find the kind of work that she wanted. At that time, I was interested in writing a novel centered on the Pentecostal movement and felt that by getting to know Lynn better that I would be able to study how that form of Christianity affected young black women. Because I had grown up in a more traditional Baptist church, I was not familiar with the charismatic nature of that branch of Christianity. After all, Lynn could speak in tongues and could get herself into a trance at any time she chose. She invited me to spend the night and we began to spend more and more time together. Lynn also asked me to help her pay her rent, help her find a car, get her nails and eyebrows done, and give her spending money. On the other hand she did not want me to interact with the rest of her family and after an initial period in which I thought we were very close she wanted to only see me during business hours and wanted her evenings to herself.

We stayed together for about 18 months. I became very fond of Jasmine and thought that my relationship with Lynn had the possibility of leading to something more permanent. One evening Lynn called and said that she wanted to have dinner because she had something very important to tell me. She told me that she had become pregnant, and I was not the daddy. Lynn had met Quincy and she said in a moment of passion that only occurred on one occasion that she became pregnant. While I was not convinced that all that she was saying was true, Lynn was asking whether I could help her to determine what to do about her pregnancy. She wanted to know whether I would condone her having an abortion. She wanted to discuss whether we could continue our relationship, or whether she should marry Quincy. Looking back at the situation it is now clear that Lynn was trying to play me, had no intention of continuing our relationship, but would continue to ask me for money even though she had decided to marry Quincy.

By that time, I had helped Lynn get into college, and had helped her with her tuition. She wanted to pursue a degree in divinity with the hopes of becoming a pastor. I always wondered how being a Pentecostal allowed her to make the decisions that she made and feel no remorse in the way that she treated people. Later, after she graduated from Luther Rice College in Lithonia, she went to graduate school and according to her, received a PhD in psychology. She told me recently that her clinical specialty is the treatment of homosexuals who have psychological difficulties.

Angela

Soon after I found out that Lynn had married Quincy (a fact that she often denied), Lynn's cousin, Londra, called me and asked if I would please help her sister who was in the midst of a difficult divorce. Lynn's cousin, Angela, was married to Lloyd Foster, also known as "Pretty Boy," in and around the Vine City section of Atlanta's West End, one of the rougher neighborhoods in Atlanta. Angela had four children, the youngest of which was less than one-year-old. Angela had run away from living with my former client Shirley when she was 13 years old. She said that she tried to prostitute herself and had a narrow escape from being killed one night when she was picked up walking on Candler Road. While she was trying to find a place to stay, she met a man from out of town whose name she cannot remember. She stayed with him for a few weeks before he left town. Angela became pregnant with her first child by this unknown man when she was 14 years old. Angela's mother, Linda, had been killed when Angela was five years old, she did not know who her natural father was, but a white man named Randy would come to visit and would on occasions sexually assault Angela. Later Randy would also engage in the same activities with one of Angela's younger cousins.

Angela went back home to Shirley's house but was unable to deal with Shirley's constant scolding and recrimination. Lynn offered to take Angela in while she was pregnant, and they lived near Six Flags. They did not get along very well, and Angela move back in with Shirley around the time of the birth of her daughter, India. Angela would often leave her baby in the care of Shirley while she went back on the streets. Shirley reported Angela to DEFACS, and the state removed India from Angela's care. Angela met another young man who she lived with for a short time. After a while Angela's new young man sold Angela to Pretty Boy. Pretty Boy was in his 30s and Angela had just turned 15. Pretty Boy offered to -help Angela regain custody of her daughter India. Pretty Boy asked Shirley if she would sign to allow Pretty Boy to marry Angela so that they could petition DEFACS to get India back. They married, India came to live with them, and when Angela was 17, she gave birth to a second daughter who they named Lloyd Foster Junior. They referred to this new child as June-June because she was a junior. When Angela was 19, she gave birth to her son who they named Lloyd Foster III. Because he looked like a Mexican when he was born, he was called Toco. When Angela was 21, she gave birth to a third daughter whose name is Isabella. By the time that Isabella was born Angela and Pretty Boy were having major difficulties. Pretty Boy did not want to stay at home while Angela was pregnant, and he would often visit another cousin of Angela's whose nickname was "Fat" by other family members. Rumors also circulated within the family that Pretty Boy was also involved with Angela's sister who was called "Baby Cakes" within the family.

Soon after Isabella was born, Angela and Pretty Boy got into a physical fight and Pretty Boy kicked Angela in the chest. In retaliation Angela doused Pretty Boy with lighter fluid but was unable to finish the deal. Pretty Boy had Angela arrested and accused her of attempted arson, Pretty Boy also took out a TPO (temporary protective order). After Angela was arrested, she spent a few days in the Fulton County Jail which is also referred to as "Rye Street" even though the jail is located on Rice Street. When Angela was released on bond, Pretty Boy called her and asked her to come home. He became very friendly, and they went into the bedroom and had sex. While she was still asleep Pretty Boy called the police and reported that she had violated the TPO and wanted to have her arrested again. The police came to the door and Pretty Boy ushered them into the bedroom where Angela was naked. Even though the situation was embarrassing and intended by Pretty Boy to dehumanize Angela, the police refused to arrest her, sensing that he had intentionally set her up.

Angel's sister, Londra, brought her to my office. Angela was very shy and did not know what to think about the possibility of my representation of her. When Angela came to see me, her four children were in the custody of Pretty Boy. Pretty Boy had filed a divorce proceeding in which he asked the court to award him permanent custody of the children. He also asked for child support and by the time that Angela had made it to my office; she had been ordered to pay monthly child support to Pretty Boy. I decided to try to help Angela even though I knew that I would not be compensated. By the time that Angela came to my office I had been representing that family for approximately 25 years and sometimes you get involved with the family and try to represent their interest as best as you can even though you know that you become vulnerable and are often second-guessed.

I quickly filed a response to Pretty Boy's complaint for divorce in which I also filed a counterclaim on behalf of Angela seeking custody of the children, alimony and property division. When Angela came to live with Pretty Boy, Pretty Boy's mother and his grandmother also lived there. According to Angela, Pretty Boy's mother suffered from dementia was unable to fully care for herself and Angela would often fight with her mother-in-law and be required to clean up her messes. Pretty Boy supported the family by giving tattoos to underage children and also selling weed. Pretty Boy had spent several years in prison where he learned how to give tattoos. Angela said that Pretty Boy had cameras all over the house and yard so that he would know if he was under surveillance by the police. Soon after I took the case a hearing was set in Superior Court. Angela had no way to get to the courthouse, so I drove to Shirley's house and picked her up. After the hearing that allowed Angela to have visitation with her children, I took her back to Shirley's and we agreed that we would have dinner that evening. Angela had an athletic body and had the mannerisms of a child. Angela confided in me that she was having real difficulties in living in the basement of Shirley's house. The basement had mold and mildew and it was making her sick. She was not happy to bring her children to her basement apartment as she felt that because of the limited space and mildew that the children would be subject to sickness. At that time, I had a two-bedroom apartment in Decatur. I told Angela that she could bring her children to my apartment, and I would move out and stay in a hotel while she was having her visitation with her four children. I also let Angela use my car. I later found out that she did not have a driver's license. Fortunately, she was able to pick up her children and return them to Pretty Boy's without incident. It was not long after that that Angela decided to move in with me. I knew it was a mistake, but I also felt sorry for her and believed that it was better for her to stay with me than wander the streets in the West End.

At the hearing, the court ordered that guardian ad litem be appointed to make a home study and determine whether it was in the best interest of the children to remain with Pretty Boy or to be in Angela's custody. During the guardian ad litem interview with Angela that occurred at my office, he asked her what her children enjoyed doing. She told him about India's activities, June June's disabilities and how "Taco love to play with toys". When the guardian asked Angela about Isabella, Angela said, "she a baby". Again, the guardian asked what Isabella liked. Because Angela had been forced out of the home because of her troubled relationship with Pretty Boy when Isabella was only a few months old, Angela had not spent enough time with her youngest daughter to get to know her very well. All she really knew about Isabella was that she was very light-skinned, and Angela would often call Isabella "my Redbone baby". The guardian's report was sent to the court in August 2009. The court-appointed guardian determined that Angela's children would be better off in her care because the neighborhood in which Pretty Boy lived was crime-ridden. Of interest was the fact that Pretty Boy was able to keep the nature of his business secret.

Because Angela had no place to go, and because I felt it was my Christian duty to help, I rented a house in Scottsdale and Angela her children and me moved in together. We had a four bedroom, 3 ½ bathroom three-story house. My bedroom was on the first floor and Angela and her children stayed on the second floor. The basement was set up for a game room and eventually the children's pet rabbit occupied that area. When Christmas time came around Pretty Boy had the children for the first week of the holidays. Angela and I decided to take a short trip to Las Vegas. Angela had never been on an airplane and had only left Georgia on one occasion to visit her brother in Alabama. Needless to say she was quite excited. After we are at stayed in Las Vegas for a day or two we decided that we would take a side trip to the Grand Canyon. We rented a car and off we went.

Everything was fine until we got past Hoover dam. The weather had been pleasant enough in Las Vegas but as we started to drive on I- 20 we soon ran into snow. All the sudden the traffic came to a stop because there had been an accident in front of us. We thought that we could bypass the traffic jam on I-20 by heading south until we could find an acceptable road to lead us back to the north on the other side of where the wreck was. We did in fact find an interstate road that headed north towards Sonoma Arizona. The further north we went we also increased the altitude and soon we were again stuck in a snowstorm. We barely made it to Sonoma, decided to have dinner and determine what we should do after that. It was clear that the best thing to do was to turn around and try to make it back to Las Vegas. As soon as we got back in the car Angela fell asleep. I do not know if she was just afraid because of all the snow in the mountains that we were driving through, or she was actually tired. I do not know how we made it down out of those mountains that evening or even how we got all the way back to Las Vegas in one piece, but we did. When it came time to return to Atlanta the next day, we overslept and missed our flight. We were sitting in the airport for several hours.

Yehuda and Stillwater

As we were waiting for the next flight, I received a call from Yehuda who had been locked out of his office because of a dispute with his partner. Yehuda had entered into an agreement with Stillwater Asset-Backed Fund a company that was in the business of making loans to lawyers. The agreement with Stillwater required Yehuda to pledge all of his assets in return for a revolving line of credit. He had to agree that he would allow Stillwater to monitor his cases and that Yehuda would assign his entire attorney's fees to Stillwater. In exchange for those pledges Stillwater agreed to provide for all of Yehuda's office expenses and allow him to draw down a monthly amount to pay his living expenses.

After I left Yehuda in 2005, he continued to maintain his office in Marietta but then at Stillwater's suggestion he entered into an agreement with another attorney, Robert Weiss, to share office space in the Galleria office complex in Cobb County. Weiss is a Hasidic Jew whose office was in New York. Weiss was also funded by Stillwater and had entered into an agreement similar to the one that Yehuda had entered into. In 2008 Yehuda and Weiss opened an office under the name of Weiss and Associates, LLC. Weiss remained in New York and Yehuda ran the office at the Galleria. The firm continued to use Yehuda's telephone number that he had been using for more than 20 years. By the time that Yehuda called me just before Christmas, 2009 the relationship between Yehuda and Weiss had soured to the point that Weiss locked Yehuda out of the office and would not allow Yehuda to access his files or use his long-standing telephone number.

When Yehuda called me while I was waiting for my flight back to Atlanta from Las Vegas, he wanted me to discuss with him how to obtain a Temporary Restraining Order (TRO) in order to gain access to his files and the office. While I was on hold at the Las Vegas airport, I walked Yehuda through the process of drafting a complaint and motion for TRO. We discussed the process of how to go about getting himself back into possession of his office and files. To Yehuda's credit, he was able to track down a Superior Court Judge on Christmas Eve in Atlanta and obtain the court order that he needed in order to get back into his office.

When Angela and I got back to Atlanta, we immediately went to Walmart to finish our Christmas shopping. We were actually there when the store closed. We went home and giftwrapped all the children's presents and got ready to pick them up the next morning. To our amazement the next day it actually snowed in Atlanta, a rarity in and of itself, but for it to happen on Christmas was quite unique. When it snows in Atlanta everything shuts down. The city is not prepared for icy roads and because Atlanta is a major trucking hub, when 18 wheelers are out on the interstates and there is ice on the roads it creates an impossible driving hazard. In fact, it wouldn't matter if the state had the same snow removal equipment as is available in Minnesota, because when a large numbers of 18 wheelers meet with on icy roads, traffic fails to move. I have now lived in Atlanta for 47 years and every time there is ice on the roads everything shuts down.

Ladder Case

While I was out of the office during the 2009 Christmas break, Joe Weeks was in the office and received a call from a new client who was looking for me. The new client explained that her husband, Sam, had fallen off of a ladder while he was doing electrical work at a business on Candler Road. The client's husband had rented an extension ladder from Home Depot and was attempting to install a connection box in an automobile collision center. The 24-foot Warner extension ladder slid out from under our client's husband, and he landed headfirst on a concrete floor. Sam suffered a severe brain injury and was being treated at Atlanta Medical Center (formerly Georgia Baptist Hospital). Joe signed up the client, informed me that we were going to work on this case together and filled me in on the details as much as he was able.

We tracked down the ladder, took possession of it, and stored it in one of those public storage bins. I called an engineering expert that I had used in previous cases for the purpose of examining the ladder to determine whether any defect in labeling or a physical defect concerning the manufacturer or lease of the ladder may have contributed to the fall. Our expert quickly pointed out that the ladder was defective because one the feet of the ladder were missing the rubber shoe that was designed to prevent the ladder from sliding, especially on a concrete surface. Within a few days we determined that we had a very good claim against Home Depot for renting a defective ladder and quickly filed a complaint in the State Court of DeKalb County. The case was assigned to Judge Johnny Panos. We included with the complaint a set of interrogatories and request for production of documents including copies of all videos in Home Depot's possession that would show the condition of the ladder at the time that it was rented by Sam. As the evidence developed, I came to believe that the lack of the rubber footing had caused the ladder to shift under our client's weight and caused Sam to fall. In a products liability case, like the one in which we were involved, once it is established that the ladder was defective (and a lack of a rubber footing was an obvious defect) then all we had to prove was that the defect was a contributing cause to the injury.

Sam was severely injured. He remained in a coma for several months and was attended to by his wife who went to the hospital on a daily basis. The doctor's diagnosis was that Sam suffered from severe trauma to the brain. He hovered between life and death for many weeks. After Sam was out of danger and he was not subject to death, he began the long process of rehabilitation. The severity of the brain injury indicated that there was permanent brain damage, and that Sam would be impaired for the remainder of his life.

We worked diligently on this case, pressed Home Depot's attorneys to provide the information that we had requested in our initial interrogatories and request to produce (RPD's). At some point in the litigation, we filed a motion in which we contended that Home Depot was withholding vital information from us and contended that we were entitled to a finding that Home Depot had spoliated evidence. Judge Panos found that Home Depot had spoliated the evidence by refusing to provide videos that would have proven the condition of the ladder at the time that it was rented by Sam. Shortly after we received that finding by the court Home Depot asked that the case be mediated. Courts usually insist that parties to litigation engage in mediation in order to try to settle their cases. In this situation the parties agreed to mediate the case by hiring a well-known mediation firm and each side went to the mediation offices in order to negotiate. Generally mediation follows a set pattern. After the obligatory greetings, the initial stage of the mediation process allows the plaintiff's lawyer to outline his client's case including the theory of liability and the damages that the client is seeking. By the time that we went to mediation we had gathered sufficient evidence to establish liability and our client had incurred more than $400,000 worth of medical bills. Initially we demanded $15 million, and Home Depot offered $150,000.

After each side had made their opening statements and initial offers, each side went into a separate room and the mediator went back and forth between the respective sides conveying offers until either the parties agree on an amount or until it becomes clear that the parties cannot come to a resolution of the case. In our particular case after a full day of going back and forth with offers and counter offers, we were still very far apart, and the mediation adjourned without the case being resolved.

As a part of the litigation process, we had scheduled to take the deposition of a representative from the Warner ladder company, the company that actually manufactured the ladder, in Chicago. The deposition was scheduled during the week between Christmas and New Year. I had never been to downtown Chicago and neither had Joe Weeks. We flew to Chicago's Midway Airport, got on the L and made our way to the loop. We were unprepared for the snow and cold wind that was coming off the lake. We eventually found the office where the deposition was to take place, thawed ourselves out and started the deposition. We were able to establish the evidence that we thought we needed to use at trial and were very excited with the testimony that we received from Warner's expert.

After the deposition we had a few hours of time in downtown Chicago and decided to walk from the office where the deposition was taken out to the lakefront. I recalled that the well-known column writer for the Atlanta Constitution, Lewis Grizzard, had been a sportswriter in Chicago for the Tribune. When Grizzard returned to the South he described Chicago as having two seasons, "the Fourth of July and winter." We certainly experienced winter in Chicago that afternoon.

It wasn't long after we took the deposition of Warner's expert that we received a call from Home Depot's attorney for the purpose of renewing settlement discussions. This time we were armed with not only an order from the court determining that Home Depot had spoliated evidence but also testimony from Warner's expert that was very favorable to our case. The case settled for a substantial amount of money. Every time I am close to a truck carrying ladders, I observe whether the extension ladder on the truck has rubber footings in place.

HTTP v. Kimberly-Clark

Yehuda had asked me to become involved with him in a case against Kimberly-Clark. Our client, HTTP, a company located in Israel had developed a heating blanket to be used during surgical procedures. Surgical procedures are categorized by the length of time required for the patient to stay in the operating room. Surgical procedures of a short duration generally do not require the use of an external source to warm the patient. Procedures lasting more than an hour require a method of warming. There are two alternative types of products used to warm patients. For surgical procedures that last more than three hours the patient is warmed by circulating water. For the intermediary procedure the warming technique is warmed air circulated around the patient. Our client, HTTP, was headquartered in Jerusalem, and had developed a warming blanket that used low-voltage electrical current to warm the patient. The warming blanket had a unique algorithm that allowed the warming blanket to use a small amount of current to achieve the temperatures desired to keep the patient warm and in addition could be used both with direct current and alternating current. The battery supply that produces the direct current also allowed the warming blanket to continue to perform while the patient was being transferred from the operating theater to the recovery unit. Our client's owner, whose name was Dorith, was very enthusiastic about the potential for this product and had obtained patents in Europe and in the United States for the device. Dorith contacted Kimberly-Clark for the purpose of determining whether Kimberly-Clark would have interest in marketing her warming blanket technology.

Initially Kimberly-Clark was interested in entering into an agreement in which HTTP would provide to Kimberly-Clark samples of the warming blankets and provide the technical information that would be needed for Kimberly-Clark to determine the feasibility of the manufacturer and sale of the warming blankets to medical providers. Kimberly-Clark had a patient warming product that used warmed circulating water for long-term surgical procedures but did not have a warming device that could be used for the less extensive surgical procedures. HTTP's product could be used for short duration, medium and long-term surgeries and therefore could potentially compete with the product that Kimberly-Clark was already marketing. One of Kimberly-Clark's product evaluators had written a memorandum in which he contended that HTTP's product was a disruptive (meaning that the technology of the HTTP warming blanket would disrupt the current technology and cause a change in patient warming methods) innovation in the patient warming product category. In addition, Medicare administrators had determined that even in short-term medical procedures that patient warming was necessary, therefore expanding the market for patient warming devices.

Kimberly-Clark's evaluation of HTTP's patient warming device came to a conclusion without a commitment from Kimberly-Clark to market HTTP's product and Kimberly-Clark informed Dorith of their decision to terminate their relationship. A few months later however, Kimberly-Clark again contacted Dorith and requested additional samples of the warming blankets and the control unit that monitored the patient temperature and sent the requisite amount of current to the warming device to keep the patient at a steady temperature. When Kimberly-Clark received the additional samples, they attempted to reverse engineer the product and make their own prototype. Kimberly-Clark then initiated a product testing seminar in which they invited potential users of the warming blanket to determine whether it was feasible to market. After determining the potential market Kimberly-Clark again informed Dorith of Kimberly-Clark's lack of interest. Dorith asked Kimberly-Clark to return the product samples that she had provided to them. Kimberly-Clark failed to return all of the samples and did not disclose that they had reverse engineered the product and had made their own prototype.

Yehuda had initially sought the help of another group of lawyers to sue Kimberly-Clark for what he perceived as a breach of contract on Kimberly-Clark's part related to the initial agreements entered into between Kimberly-Clark and H TTP. A suit was filed in the Superior Court of Fulton County. The agreement between Yehuda and the other attorneys required that Yehuda fund the litigation and when a controversy arose between Yehuda and the other group of attorneys, the other attorneys decided to withdraw from the litigation. At that point Yehuda asked me to get involved with the case. I was somewhat reluctant to get into a case involving product development, patents, and foreign nationals with whom I had never communicated. On the other hand I was already involved with Yehuda in his case against Weiss and Stillwater and thought that I had sufficient resources to get involved in the HTTP case. I asked Joe Weeks to assist me and because we had just finished the case against Home Depot he decided to get involved.

Yehuda Smolar immigrated to the United States from Israel with his parents. He went to high school in Hartford, Connecticut and then attended the University of Connecticut. After graduation he found a job with AIG as a commercial insurance adjuster. Yehuda worked in North Carolina for several years before coming to Atlanta. I first met Yehuda while he was still working at AIG and his wife was being represented by Jim Ritchie when I was at Jesse Ritchie and Duncan. Yehuda decided to go to law school and attended John Marshall School of Law. Soon after graduation he set up his own firm to handle mainly personal injury cases. Yehuda hired Barry Roseman who had been one of the associates at Jesse Ritchie and Duncan. Yehuda was able to get high end personal injury cases because of his relationship with a prominent neurosurgeon that referred brain injury cases to him. It wasn't long before Yehuda had started to make a good living by settling the cases that he had gotten as a result of his relationships with doctors. Unfortunately, despite the fact that Yehuda had made significant money he generally spent more money than he made. When his marriage to his first wife came to an end, he met Amy, married her and within a short time they had three children. Amy was not Jewish but converted so that their children would be raised in the Jewish faith.

Amy would often show up at Yehuda's office and order the secretaries around. After being married for several years, the marriage started to disintegrate, and Yehuda and Amy went through a difficult divorce. During one extended visitation session Yehuda took the children on a cruise and while on that cruise, Yehuda met JoJo. Before long Yehuda and JoJo were an item. On occasions JoJo would show up at the office in her micro miniskirt clomping down the hall in her high heels. The lawyers and the secretaries often would gossip about JoJo especially concerning the time at the annual Christmas party that she had had more than a few too many and entertained the group by insisting on singing along with the karaoke machine.

The HTTP case required extensive research and writing. Kimberly-Clark was represented by Bryan Cave, a major national firm that has offices throughout the United States and in several foreign countries. I dug into the evidence, requested production of documents, and had extensive discussions with our clients in Jerusalem. The work was very demanding it required my attention almost to the exclusion of any other case that I was working on. I had to prepare and take many depositions, struggled to understand patent law and deal with clients that were very difficult not only to understand, but who made unrealistic demands. After more than a year of digging into the facts and law, we were able to get an offer of settlement after a mediation session, but the client refused any settlement offer. Shortly thereafter, Kimberly-Clark filed a motion for summary judgment. The judge handling the case, after remarking that the court's file was the largest in the courthouse, granted Kimberly-Clark's motion and after an attempted appeal the case came to a close. During that time, I had almost worked exclusively on the H TTP case to the detriment of my practice.

Mother's Stroke

In late July 2013 my mother had a stroke. Mother suffered from arterial fibrillation (a-fib), a condition that makes your heartbeat irregularly. Her doctor initially prescribed Coumadin because a-fib can and often does create blood clots that can migrate through the blood system to the brain and cause a stroke. When taking Coumadin, the patient is required to have their INR level (a measure of the viscosity of the blood) checked on a regular basis. When taking Coumadin, you are advised not to drink alcohol or to eat leafy green vegetables except occasionally. My mother was doing fine taking the Coumadin, but she did not like the fact that she could not eat green leafy vegetables and asked her doctor if there was some other blood thinner that she could take. At the time my mother was 86 years old and in fairly good health except for the a-fib. Mother's doctor prescribed Pradaxa: another blood thinner that did not require constant monitoring and allowed people to eat green leafy vegetables. However, Pradaxa I later found out should not be given to individuals who are over 75 years old.

I would regularly visit my mother and I believe that she always enjoyed my visits especially after my father had died. The last time I visited my mother at her home, as I was getting ready to leave when my mother had a severe nosebleed. I stayed with her until she was able to get the nosebleed under control. She said that she had been having some difficulty with nosebleeds, but her doctor did not change her prescription for the Pradaxa. A month or so later mother had another very severe nosebleed and she had to be taken by ambulance to the hospital. Her doctor after that episode took her off the Pradaxa and would only allow her to take a baby aspirin even though her a-fib condition could cause blood clots and therefore strokes. Within two weeks after her doctor took her off the Pradaxa mother had a severe stroke. My sister had been talking to Mother on the telephone when my mother said that she was very dizzy and that she was experiencing some problems. My sister called our cousin who lives next door to my mother, and he immediately came over, called an ambulance and my mother was taken to the nearest emergency room which happens to be on Fort Bragg. Cathy called me and told me what was going on and within an hour I was on the road to North Carolina.

When I arrived at the hospital about six hours later mother was in bed, was able to recognize me and was able to speak to me albeit with a slurred speech. Her doctor said that she had gotten mother up that mother was somewhat impaired on her right side but had been doing somewhat better from the time when she had come into the hospital. I stayed with mother for the rest of the day and that evening went to mother's house for the evening. When I came back to the hospital the next morning mother was undergoing several tests to determine the extent and severity of the stroke. The testing procedures exhausted my mother, and she went into a deep sleep after the technicians had finished with sonograms and other testing. When mother finally woke up, she was no longer able to speak, she was unable to use her right arm and right leg and she had such a blank stare that I became aware that she did not recognize me. Cathy was unable to come to North Carolina for a couple of weeks and so I stayed there to attend to my mother until Cathy could get there. Mother's condition seemed to worsen to the extent that she did not recognize me, could not speak, did not recognize the visitors that came to see her and could not even feed herself.

After being at Womack Army Hospital for a month, mother was transferred to a rehabilitation facility in Fayetteville, North Carolina. Cathy could not stay with mother for a long period of time, so I again went to North Carolina and stayed with my mother at the hospital for another month or more. Needless to say my law practice suffered a great deal. My attention to my cases suffered, work that needed to get done was neglected, and the attorneys in my office and my secretary also seemed to go on vacation because nothing seemed to get done in my absence. While I was attending to my mother, the office location changed. My secretary was supposed to make sure that my files and my office equipment were moved to the new location. When I finally returned to the office my desk had been destroyed in the move, my files were scattered, things that were in my office were lost and my ability to deal with the transition was very much hampered. I lost all the momentum I had gained prior to my mother's illness and had trouble merely keeping up with the daily grind of my law practice. I do not know if the move to the new location or the sadness of my mother's condition caused my inattention to my law practice, but the work did suffer. I was also experiencing a problem with my hip and was unable to walk without pain. All these factors I am sure contributed to my inability to adequately deal with my law practice.

My mother's health continued to fail. I told Cathy that it was necessary for us to have a guardian appointed for mother because it became clear that mother was not going to be able to return to her house and take care of herself. Cathy asked that I allow her to take on the responsibility of the guardianship and because Cathy had already retired from her job at NOAA and because I was still actively practicing law in Atlanta, I agreed that Cathy would be the best person to serve as mother's guardian. Cathy decided to have mother taken from Fayetteville to Savannah. She also decided to pack up mother's belongings and rent mother's house to our cousin.

Revolving Doors

Back in Atlanta, I was contacted by Yehuda to help him work on a case involving an injury to an older woman who was hit by the revolving door at the Four Seasons Hotel. Yehuda had moved his office to a location near Atlantic Station in Midtown Atlanta. His office was in an old warehouse building that had been refurbished and at one time had been a recording studio. There was an extra office because his paralegal had gotten into an argument with JoJo and decided to move on. I began to go over to Yehuda's office on a regular basis to work on the Four Seasons case. I would go to my office in Decatur and then go across town to Yehuda's office. After a while my time at the office in Decatur became less and less and eventually, I made a permanent move to the Midtown office.

The Four Seasons case involved a revolving door that was activated by a motion sensor. When someone came in the vicinity of the revolving door it started to move and continued to move while the person was in the confines of the revolving door. Anna Enríquez was injured when struck by the automated revolving door installed at the Four Seasons Hotel on 14th Street in Atlanta on July 11, 2011. The revolving door is a powered door manufactured by Horton Automatics a division of Overhead Doors. The door was installed at the Four Seasons by an authorized representative of Overhead Doors. Automated Door Ways was the authorized representative of Over Head Doors. Automated Door Ways preformed maintenance service on the revolving door. Additionally, ASSA Abloy Door Group preformed maintenance services on the door and was called on by Four Seasons to inspect and maintain the door during the significant time periods of time that were related to this case. Nghi Mai inspected and preformed maintenance services on the revolving door on behalf of ASSA Abloy during the time relevant to this case.

Anna Enríquez was an invitee of the Four Seasons Hotel. Enríquez had dinner at the restaurant located in the Four Seasons Hotel with friends and was departing the hotel through the revolving door at the main entrance of the hotel. While Enríquez was traveling through the door trying to exit the hotel she was struck from behind by one of the components of the door, knocked to the ground and injured. Enríquez suffered a broken hip, immediate pain and suffering, shock and fright. Ms. Enríquez was transported to the emergency room, hospitalized and had to undergo surgery caused by the injuries she received as a result of being struck by the defective revolving door. Enríquez accumulated more than $45,000 in medical expenses and had to be cared for as a result of her injuries.

The Revolving door, sometimes referred to as a Horton Revolver, was installed at the Four Seasons Hotel in 1990. The door was manufactured by the Horton Division of Overhead Doors. The door is an automatic four wing door that has a motion sensor that causes the door to start to spin when it detects that a person is approaching the door. The door moves in a counter clockwise motion and continues to move until the sensor does not detect any further motion to activate the door. When the door was manufactured, it came with warning decals that warned users that the door would not stop and that users of the door should not stop moving until they had passed through the door. The door had a safety switch that would cause the door to stop if an object was caught between the door wing and the door housing. The only other safety feature that the door came equipped with was a potentiometer, a sensor that detected that the wings of the door had come in contact with an object and that the back pressure on the door that was sufficient to cause the door to stop. The manufacturer recommended that the potentiometer be set so that the door would stop if the back pressure on the door wing was greater than 15 lbs. After the door was installed, the manufacturer developed and marketed a retro fit for the door that would sense that a person traversing through the door had slowed down or stopped while inside the revolving door. This retrofit was available for the door in question before Enríquez was injured.

While the warning labels that came with the door were available for use with this revolving door from the time of the door's instillation, Four Seasons determined that the warning labels were not aesthetically pleasing and refused to place the warning labels on the door and continued to refuse to place the warning labels on the door during the times relevant to the case. Both ASSA Abloy and Automated Door Ways are members of the American Association of Automatic Door Manufactures (AAADM) and subscribe to the standards of the AAADM and ANSI (American National Standards Institute) related to the maintenance and servicing of the revolving door in question in this case. Those standards, applicable to those servicing the automatic revolving door in this case and the owner of the door, require that the owner of the door cause the door to be put out of service if the door does not meet the minimal standards stated in the AAADM and ANSI publications. The technician working for ASSA Abloy stated that he knew that the door in question did not have the warning labels that are prescribed by those standards and that the owner (Four Seasons) should have been instructed to take the door out of service until the warning labels were placed on the door. That technician, Nghi Mai, stated that he did not tell the management of the Four Seasons to shut the automatic revolving door down. Additionally, while both ASSA Abloy and Automated Door Ways knew that a retro fit was available to provide an additional safety device to users of the automatic revolving door in this case, neither servicing company provided Four Seasons with the details of the availability of the retro fit.

After Enríquez was injured a representative of Overhead Doors inspected the automatic revolving door at the Four Seasons and found that the potentiometer setting on the automatic revolving door at the Four Seasons was greater than 60 lbs. of back pressure. That representative could not determine the actual setting because the measuring device only measured up to 60 lbs. Neither of the service technicians employed by ASSA Abloy or Automated Door Ways knew what the setting for the potentiometer was because they had never tested the device and never tried to set the limits of the potentiometer.

I did most of the work on the Enríquez case. I wrote all of the briefs, took all the depositions, prepared the case for trial and did everything necessary to make sure that the case was ready for when it was called for trial. At the outset of the case Yehuda had promised that I would receive 50% of any fee that was generated either by trial or settlement. I wrote a memo to that effect and put it in Yehuda's hand.

The defendants asked that the case be sent to mediation and off to mediation we went. I made the opening statement and dealt with the clients during the caucus portion of the mediation. Yehuda stationed himself in the lobby of the mediation company so that he could determine whether there were factions among the various defendants. Late in the afternoon we were able to reach a settlement in the amount of $250,000. The contingency fee on this case was 40% of the total recovery or $100,000. My portion would have been $50,000.

It took a few weeks for the money to arrive at our office. Unknown to me, Yehuda receive the money and before I knew it, he and JoJo took off for a vacation in Cyprus. When Yehuda returned, I asked him for my money, and he told me that there was another lawyer involved and that my portion would be much less than the 50% that he had initially guaranteed me. Yes, I was upset, and I decided that any further business relationship with Yehuda would be futile. He had again taken advantage of my hard work and cheated me out of my portion of the fee. To make matters worse, my mother succumbed to her stroke and died 18 months after my father had passed away.

One afternoon I received a call from a potential new client. The young lady on the telephone wanted to set up a meeting with me to discuss the potential representation of her employer. I agreed to the meeting and Nadya met me at my office to discuss her client's potential case. Nadya is a beautiful young woman that invariably makes a great first impression on anybody who meets her. Later that day I had to travel to Florida to take a deposition. I gave Nadya my cell phone number and to my surprise she called me that evening and we had a long conversation. I agreed to meet her for dinner when I returned to Atlanta. At the time of this meeting, I was still involved with Angela but my relationship with Angela was tenuous at best.

Hip Replacement

I continued to work at Yehuda's office but by November 2015 my hip had gotten to the point that I needed to have a hip replacement. My old friend Grant Brantley had to have his hip replaced and had had very good success with the procedure. His doctor came highly recommended, and I decided that I would use Dr. Dysart to replace my left hip. My pre-op examination revealed that I had extensive arthritic damage to both hips and both of my knees. I decided that my best course of action was to have my left hip replaced followed by replacement of my right knee, left knee and finally right hip.

I went to the hospital on November 7, 2015, for left hip replacement surgery. After I came out of the surgery, I had no more pain in my left hip and felt extremely happy. I got up that evening and was able to walk with the assistance of a walker. I left the hospital the next day and decided to keep off my feet for a few days. By the next weekend I felt strong enough to use the walker to walk about a block to get to my car and retrieve the literature that I needed in order to teach the Sunday school lesson that weekend. My left leg was doing okay but I started to feel a little pain just below my hip. Everything seemed to be going well and I decided that by the following week I could return to the office and get some work accomplished.

I was scheduled for hearing in the Superior Court of Cobb County on December 7. I walked down to my car and as I was getting into my car something snapped in my left leg and I felt like I had been shot. I was able to drive to my office and struggled to get out of my car and into the lobby of the office. I called the court and reported that I was unable to attend the hearing because I believed that I had broken my leg and that I was going to see my doctor. I got the receptionist to drive me to my doctor's office. I struggled again to get out of the car and up to the doctor's reception area. Dr. Dysart was out of town, and I was seen by his PA. An x-ray confirmed that I had broken the top of my left femur where the metal shaft of the hip replacement was located. The PA got me a prescription for painkillers and sent me home. She told me that I would be scheduled for surgery for the following Monday. I stayed in bed writhing in pain all weekend. On Sunday night I received a call from Dr. Dysart who wanted to know why he could not find me at the hospital. I told him that his PA had sent me home and that I was to come back to the hospital Monday afternoon.

When Monday finally rolled around, I got my son to drive me to Kenestone Hospital in Marietta. My pain level had been off the chart all weekend and I was relieved when I was finally given a knockout shot before going back into surgery. Dr. Dysart told my son that the metal shaft that extended into my femur was not long enough and that he had to replace that part of the prosthesis. I remained in the hospital overnight and at about 11 PM that evening Dr. Dysart came into my room for a post-op check. Dr. Dysart told me that the muscles in my leg were so thick that it took him an extra-long period of time to put the first metal part into my leg and that because of the problem that I had that I was no longer a candidate for any further surgery affecting my left hip. Needless to say, I had a bad experience, and that experience was about to get worse.

It took me an extra-long period of time to recover from the two surgeries that I had had on my left hip within about four weeks of each other. I had gotten extremely behind on the work that I was doing and was not getting any help from any source. When I was finally able to get to the office, I had to be driven and assisted to get out of the car, climbed the steps and finally make it to my office. Additionally, I was still in some pain and found it hard to concentrate. I would tire out very easily and I needed to go home after just a few hours of being in the office. It took me several months in order to start to feel better but by then I was having difficulties with keeping up with the work that I needed to accomplish on behalf of my clients.

After several months of recuperating from the two hip surgeries I noticed that the surgical wound at the site of the hip replacement was turning red and my left leg was swelling. After several more months I decided that I would seek medical advice but decided that I should not go back to Dr. Dysart. I was seen by my regular doctor who examined the wound and told me that he was afraid that an infection had set in at the site of my hip replacement. My doctor sent me to an infectious disease doctor to determine the particulars of the infection. The results were that I had a staph infection that was of an aggressive nature and that I needed to schedule a third hip replacement on my left hip. My general doctor recommended that I go to Emory orthopedics. It turned out that the doctor that I was referred to had been my general practitioner's friend in medical school at Duke. I was scheduled for a third surgery to have my left hip replaced in April 2017.

On the day that the third hip replacement surgery was scheduled I went to the hospital, check myself in and went into the prep room. I was separated from the patient to my right by a curtain and I could hear the discussion that was going on in that room. The woman next to me was having her left leg amputated because of an infection that had set in as a result of a knee of replacement. I was not encouraged about my own need for an operation based on what I heard in the room next to where I was being prepared.

Finally, it was my turn, and I was told that I would be receiving a temporary hip replacement that included a prosthesis that was filled with an antibiotic that would eliminate the infection from which I was suffering. I was put to sleep and when I awoke that evening everything seemed to be in order, and I went to sleep believing that I had finally come to the end of my problems concerning my left hip replacement.

When I had gone into the hospital my vital signs indicated that my creatinine level (a measurement of the effectiveness of my kidney function) was exactly where it should be at 0.7. By the morning after the surgery my curative level began to rise, and a host of other doctors began to visit me in my hospital room. Over the next few days my creatinine level continued to rise, and it finally topped out at 7.7. I remained in the hospital for one month while the doctors determined whether or not I needed to be put on dialysis. During that time, I was taken from the Emory orthopedic Hospital to the Emory hospital main campus for the purpose of having a pic line put into my chest in order to deliver the antibiotics that the infectious disease doctors determined that I needed. Because I had previously had blood clots in my chest the doctors were unable to accomplish the placement of a pic line. Eventually a port was placed in my left arm in order to deliver the antibiotics that were prescribed. I was finally released from the hospital a month after I had entered for my third hip replacement. I took a hotel room close to the hospital so that I could be checked on a daily basis by a visiting nurse. After another month of not being able to work or do anything else I was finally relieved to be able to have the port in my arm removed.

One of the problems that I was experiencing during this time was that when my kidneys were being impaired while I was still in the hospital, I was unable to urinate. By the time I got out of the hospital the exact opposite problem was occurring. I could not go very far away from the bathroom and had an abundance of urine. I was unable to go out in the evenings for fear of wetting myself. Finally, I decided to travel to Meldrim, Georgia to stay with my sister. I arrived in early June, immediately had to take a shower and change my clothes because I was unable to make it from Atlanta to her house without overflowing my undergarments. I remained at my sister's house with her, her husband Chris and her mother-in-law Christine until near the end of July.

Nuisance

After I had been in Cathy's for a few days she told me that she was experiencing difficulty with her neighbors. One of her neighbors would burn garbage in his yard, and another neighbor would spray paint for extended periods of time. Both of those neighbors were downwind of Cathy and Chris's house and therefore they were getting smoke and overspray. Chris's mother was 96 years old and suffered from a respiratory disorder. The smoke and paint fumes were causing her difficulties and were also affecting Cathy and Chris. Chris went to the neighbor that was burning garbage in his yard and knocked on his door. When he announced the purpose of his visit the neighbor slammed the door in his face and told him that they were living in the country and people can do whatever they wanted to do in their own yard. Cathy and Chris had also reported the man doing the spray painting to the local police who had put a note on the man store advising him that he was violating the local ordinances.

When the spray painting and trash burning did not stop Cathy asked me if there was anything that I could do to help the situation. I dictated a complaint alleging a continuing nuisance and told Chris how to file the complaint and seek a temporary restraining order. The county seat for Effingham County in which Cathy and Chris's house is located is Springfield, Georgia. We got a hearing before Judge F. Gates Peed within a few days and were able to convince the judge that Cathy and Chris's neighbors were violating county ordinances and that they should be stopped from burning garbage and spray painting in their yards. The judge issued a TRO and

Cathy, and Chris were greatly relieved by the outcome.

Getting the neighbors served with the nuisance complaint was another problem. The tenant that was burning the trash in the yard refused to come to the door when the sheriff tried to serve him with the complaint. We were, however, able to track down the owner of the property who lived in an adjoining County. Chris and I drove to Claxton, Georgia (also known as the fruitcake capital of the world) and engaged the Sheriff's office to serve the property owner.

Just before the case was ready to be tried, Chris's mother passed away in the trial of the case had to be postponed. The temporary restraining order is still in effect and Cathy and Chris are getting great relief from the fact that the trash burning, and the spray painting has ceased. On the other hand, shots have been fired in the direction of Cathy and Chris's house from an unknown source within the past few months.

Spiritual Warfare

When I felt well enough to travel again, I returned to Atlanta and found a new place to live. By the middle of August 2017, I was again able to return to my duties as a Sunday school teacher and resume my law practice. You may ask, and rightfully so, what does this all mean? I am not sure that I can answer with a great deal of clarity.

I have good children who profess Christ as their personal savior, but each of them has their own set of problems, and I worry about them and their relationships. I have had three failed marriages. At the same time some of my clients hate me and some of my clients love me. The Sunday school class that I teach wants to hear what I have to say on Sunday morning and Nadya, with whom I have had a relationship for the past five years, and I have become closer to marriage. On the other hand, I wonder if I were to die today whether anyone would show up at my funeral. Elaine once told me that she could not wait until I died so that she can come and spit on my grave. I have not heard from Ily for several years and have no idea about where she may be. Nick and Ali are close to their mother, perhaps closer to her than to me. But through all this I continue to believe that God is near and that I believe He knows my needs and rewards me when I diligently seek Him.

When I started law school in 1970 the Dean spoke to the incoming class and stated the age-old adage "that the law is a jealous mistress that requires all your time and effort to satisfy." Over the years I have given substantial time and effort to my law practice and have been sometimes rewarded and sometimes disappointed in pursuing cases on behalf of clients, some of whom have been greatly rewarded and some of whom have been greatly disappointed. Clients often feel that there attorney owes them a victory over every issue whether their case is just or unjust, whether they have good facts or bad facts, even whether they are innocent or guilty. It does not matter if the client is right or wrong; most times they either blame their attorney for their own failure or praise their attorney when they receive a proceeds check. Maybe we treat God in the same way. During good times we sing God's praise, but when adversity strikes, we look for an excuse to place blame.

I once represented a woman who was a speech pathologist. She was arrested because she was over-billing Medicaid and submitting fraudulent pay requests for clients for whom she had not performed services. Her personal life was troubled by a bad marriage. She had an infant child and was not receiving child support from an abusive husband. When she asked me to represent her, I advised her that her best solution was to work out a plea deal. She insisted that she was not guilty and that the state was prosecuting her because she was a black female and that other speech pathologist that were neither black nor female had similar billing practices and the state was not prosecuting them.

I demanded that she provide to me her books and records so that I could understand her billing practices and assess whether the defenses that she claimed that she had were viable. She always told me that she was going to provide the information that I was seeking and that she had witnesses who would testify on her behalf that her billing practices were acceptable amongst speech pathologist within the Atlanta metropolitan area. She continued to tell me that she was going to provide the witnesses and the documents, but she always kept putting me off and merely promising to provide the witnesses and information that I needed. After many months of trying to prepare for trial and after several plea deals had been offered by the state, the trial was set. The evidence against her was overwhelming and yet she continued to insist on her innocence. When the prosecution rested, my client insisted that she testify on her own behalf even though I recommended that she not testify. The judge in the case when I called her to the stand recessed and told my client that it was not in her best interest to testify. Still, she insisted on taking the stand. The cross-examination was withering, and she had to admit that she had cheated the state out of more than $100,000.

During the trial judge had admonished the jury not to seek outside sources regarding any matters that might be put into evidence in the case. After the testimony and argument, the jury retired and within a reasonably short period of time returned a verdict of guilty. One of the jurors prior to being dismissed gratuitously told the court that she had consulted an outside source regarding billing practices of speech pathologists. The juror admitted that in open court and prior to dismissing the jury the judge required the jury to return to the jury room and confronted the jurors outside the presence of the parties and their attorneys. These facts created an issue that potentially would require a new trial.

Based on the jury verdict the judge sentenced my client to 10 years in prison and assessed a fine in the amount that she had stolen from the state. My client asked that she be allowed to report to the jail after she had made arrangements for the care of her child and made other arrangements. The day came for her to report but she did not show up. The judge called me to the courthouse to determine if I knew the location of my client or had any information regarding her whereabouts. I had no knowledge but informed the court that she had asked me to seek a new trial because the one juror had violated the court's instructions concerning outside sources. The judge set a hearing on the motion for new trial and insisted that my client attend the motion hearing. Of course, as soon as she showed her face at the courthouse she was arrested, and the court denied her motion for new trial.

I wondered how that woman could have maintained her own belief in her own innocence. The evidence was overwhelming against her. Though she promised to provide witnesses and documents to support her case she could not do so. She even had difficulty in paying my fees. Was it her desperation that caused her to act so irrationally? Did she actually believe that a miracle would occur and that she would escape the consequences of her actions? Did she believe that I could overcome the facts and the law that were overwhelmingly against her? On the day that she was arrested and taken away by the deputy sheriffs in that courtroom in DeKalb County she blamed me.

That client's actions are not an isolated event. Over the years I have learned that people when faced with overwhelming odds against them often choose to ignore the reality of the situation and become susceptible to a belief system that either causes them to pin their hope on their religious belief, on good luck, or more often on misrepresentations made by those that seek to take advantage. I had previously mentioned the case of Annie Thomas versus The Brown Realty Company. As I mentioned before the Browns had developed a scheme to obtain the equity in the homes of individuals who are threatened by foreclosure. In the early 80s the economic conditions were very favorable for obtaining a large amount of money by engaging in what I have termed to be "foreclosure fraud". When individuals had purchased their homes in the 1960s and 1970s the interest rates for home equity loans were low and were written in such a way that the loans could be assumed by people like the Browns. This meant that the low interest loans that were initially given to the homeowner could be assumed by a purchaser. Later, the deeds to secure debt (mortgage document) contained what became known as a due on sales clause. The due on sales clause provided that if the mortgagee (usually the homeowner) sold or otherwise transferred their interest in the property that the mortgage became due in full immediately. Without that clause in the debt instrument, the Browns were free to take title to individual's property, assume the loan, refinance the property, take out the equity in the property, and move on to the next victim. This process allowed the Browns to amass a considerable amount of money. This scheme was a common practice and was the subject of a series of get rich schemes advertised on TV.

The basis for that scheme was that the homeowner who was facing foreclosure put their faith in the assurances of Gladys Brown that she was going to help the homeowner. When my clients, victims of the Brown's scheme realized what had happened to them they became angry because they realize they had been taken advantage of at a time when they were most susceptible to misrepresentations. Interestingly, all of my clients were black individuals who had worked hard to purchase a house and keep it. Many of my clients believed that the Browns had been sent to them by God in answer to their prayers.

Lack of discernment can lead to false hope and in some cases disaster.

After the Brown foreclosure fraud litigation had been resolved another scheme involving real estate in Atlanta came into my office. I previously mentioned my role in the Fleet Finance cases. Again, the economic conditions in Atlanta provided an opportunity for those that would take advantage of the poor to create a condition in which they could divest homeowners of the equity in their homes. The housing stock especially in the black communities in South Fulton, South DeKalb, Clayton and Henry County were such that the home repairs were always necessary. Companies that claimed to be home repair specialists saw an opportunity. The aforementioned movie starring Danny DeVito, *The Tin Man*, is pretty close to the actual events that allowed so-called repair companies to take advantage of the poor.

The scenario usually occurred as follows: a man from a repair company would knock on the victim's door and say, "I was doing work in your neighborhood and happened to notice that there is a problem with your roof. My company is doing work for your neighbors, and we are willing to fix your roof and you will not have to come out of pocket for any of the costs. All you need to do is to sign this document (a second mortgage on your property) and we will get to work."

The repair company, a/k/a the tin man took the mortgage document to a lender that funded the repairs. The repair company usually did very shoddy work that would not be acceptable in the industry and within a few days left the project. The initial lenders (who we later referred to as the seven dwarfs) would then sell the paper to Fleet. These second mortgage loans were for high interest rates and were very unfavorable to the homeowner. Fleet, who had originally been making consumer loans for personal property purchases to poor black people, employed an aggressive collection technique to make sure that the homeowners understood that if they did not make payments on a regular basis that they would be harassed and threatened. Many times, the harassing statement went something like this, "if you don't pay, we are going to have you arrested." That statement was usually followed by a drive-by, someone in a car with a Fleet logo on it would drive by so that the homeowner understood that they were being watched.

My client, Lily Mae Star, lived in a black enclave in that part of Cobb County that is also a part of the upscale community of Vinings. That area of the county had been settled by a community of individuals that was predominantly black. That was unusual for Vinings, but it also met the profile of those homes that were subject to the "tin man" scheme. Lily Mae needed repairs to her house and was approached by a tin man who convinced her to sign a second mortgage on her house in order to get the repairs completed. The tin man took the promissory note and second deed to secure debt to one of the seven dwarves who funded the repairs and then sold the paper to Fleet. Before long Lily Mae was receiving threats from Fleet that I considered to be extortionate. While Fleet's collectors did not threaten to break Lily Mae's leg, they certainly let her know that if she did not pay, Fleet would ruin her credit, kick her out of her house, and initiate criminal proceedings against her. Lily Mae's first instinct was to file a bankruptcy and she met with Ralph Goldbloom. Ralph called me, and I called Bill Brennan. Goldbloom worked in the office of Roy Barnes and before long we were all meeting to discuss how to handle a potential class-action. As I mentioned the case resolved itself after we were successful in getting the class certified. I received a letter from Lily Mae saying that I was the greatest lawyer in the world.

In all the cases that I have handled for these past 40+ years I have tried to do my best to represent my clients with all the skill that I can muster. Sometimes I was very successful but sometimes I failed to get the results for which I had hoped. Sometime success seemed to happen when I did not think the case merited the success that was received. At other times despite the hard work that went into the case I failed. I have questioned myself on many occasions about why one case is successful, and another is not. Often outside factors, such as unknown facts, the judge's lack of knowledge of the law, or even political affiliation affected the outcome. It is clear that predictability is elusive when trying big cases. You can only do your best and hope for the best. I wonder if our spiritual lives are equally as unpredictable.

When my son Nicholas was born in 1976, I had been a Christian for almost 20 years. I attended church regularly but had not dedicated myself to understanding the ramifications of living a Christian life. When Nick was born, and I realized that I was going to have to take care of him probably for the rest of my life. I decided it was time for me to become serious about Christianity. I began to study the Bible intently. I read it from cover to cover first in the King James version then in the Revised Standard Version. Before long I was called upon to teach Sunday school classes that also caused me to become more intensely interested in Bible study and to contemplate my role as a Christian.

It was important to me to diligently seek God's will in my life. As I had mentioned before at the end of my first year in law school, God intervened in my life by opening an opportunity to become a summer missionary in Washington DC. As a result of my time in Washington I was offered a position at a major law firm in New Orleans. Settling in New Orleans, however, did not seem to be what I was called to do. Phyllis did not want to stay in New Orleans. She had become sick and did not like being so far away from her family. An opportunity opened to us to move to Atlanta where her sister and her husband had already located. After moving we quickly became involved with an active church group of young married couples close to our own age. After being in the church for couple of years I was asked to teach an older lady Sunday school class and became involved with a group of laymen who were intent on spreading the gospel of Jesus Christ to lost people.

I cannot really remember how it was that I happen to be chosen to participate in that group, but I was asked to go on weekend revivals throughout the state of Georgia with the specific intent of seeking to offer the gospel of Jesus Christ to lost individuals. The group, known as the "lay lead revival team" consisted of a group of approximately 10 men who agreed to travel to different parts of the state, train church members on how to witness to lost people, that the church had identified, and engage in services from Friday evening until the Sunday morning service was completed. During the time that I was involved with the lay lead revival team, I met some very dedicated Christians that helped me to realize the power of Christian fellowship. It was evident that these men and women had periods in their lives that caused them to suffer. One man, who became a close friend to me, was Tex Wagstaff. Tex lived in Lizella,

Georgia. He had been a heavy equipment operator but had to retire as a result of health issues. When I met Tex, we very quickly became friends and when we were called for weekend revivals I would drive to Lizella and pick him up on the way to the revival. Tex gave his personal testimony which included a time in which he was in college, and he was convicted for having failed to live up to his Christian responsibilities. Another close friend, Bobby Burnett told how his life was changed after the death of his son in a tragic automobile accident. Others had stories of having failed in relationships, deaths of loved ones, and many other periods of suffering that they had gone through before finding a closer walk with Jesus.

It seemed that after each weekend revival my heart would be filled with joy. I would return home to my family with the desire to live a better and more dedicated Christian life. On Monday I would go to work and within a few hours there would be any number of temptations. During that time my secretary would tempt me with sexual invitations. As much as I tried to resist, I failed. The cycle of spiritual high followed by sexual temptation seem to occur over and over again. After many months of succumbing to temptations I finally decided that I had to get away. Eventually the firm fired my secretary, and I was able to resist. It was a very traumatic time in my life, spiritual highs followed by temptation and sinful conduct. I would like to say that after dealing with the temptations that had come to me that I was able to overcome through the power of the Holy Spirit acting in my life. That would be a half-truth, however. While I continue to seek God and pray that he would enable me to overcome the temptations that I faced that did not end the testing that I had to go through.

It seems to me that the spiritual warfare that goes on all around us is particularly acute with those who actively and aggressively seek God. I once read a book by Philip Yancey in which he stated that all mankind seeks to know what it is that God has to do with each of us (that specifically includes me). After reflecting on that for many years I have come to the conclusion that we all want to know first is there a God and secondly if there is a God what does he require of me. At times in my life, it has been clear God has spoken, I have heard what he has to say to me. At other times God seems distant. When God is distant from me the direction in my life seems to wander. Conflicts are most notable when I am unclear as to my purpose and direction. I think to myself "does this happen to everyone, or am I unique in the way that God is dealing with me?" Why do my prayers seem to go unanswered? I even get to the point of saying to myself am I foolish for trusting that I am a child of God, and that God cares for me. At times I seem surrounded by those who do not believe that God is in control or even that God cares. Despair and rejection have taken their toll on my life. Sometimes even in the midst of a major victory in a lawsuit that I was handling I would still feel despair.

I never felt it necessary to seek professional help when in the midst of gloom and despair. The words of Jesus, "Come unto me, all ye that labor and are heavy laden, and I will give you rest. Take my yoke upon you and learn of me; for I am meek and lowly in heart: and ye shall find rest unto your souls" Matthew 11: 28-29 would find me. While on many occasions that would not end the despair that I found myself in, eventually these words and others such as "Therefore I tell you, do not worry about your life, what you will eat or drink; or about your body, what you will wear. Is not life more than food and the body more than clothes? Look at the birds in the air; they do not sow or reap or store away in barns, and yet your heavenly Father feeds them. Are you not much more valuable than they? Can anyone of you by worrying add a single hour to your life? But seek ye first His kingdom and His righteousness, and all these things will be given to you as well. Therefore, do not worry about tomorrow, for tomorrow will worry about itself. Each day has enough trouble of its own." Matthew 6:25-34. It seemed that the more that I was able to learn about Jesus and his ministry when he was on earth that the easier it became for me to live without despair.

I did not make the choice to give up worries easily. I would often relapse. Issues with my family, the troubles that my son went through, the health of my daughter, my own financial situations continue to cause me to worry. When my marriages failed and I was alone, my heart was broken. When Ily left me, and I went through a divorce in the fall of 1992 I felt so bad that I actually crawled under my bed on Thanksgiving Day and wanted to die. It was then that I would remember going to church with my mother on Thanksgiving. Standing next to her, singing hymns, hearing the ministers giving thanks for the blessings that God had given, was a blessing. A time of praise and thanksgiving has always helped to remind me that if I seek to draw near to Jesus that he would in fact draw near to me. In Philippians 4:4-7 Paul reminds us that we should rejoice in the Lord always and that we should not worry about anything because the peace of God that surpasses all understanding will stand guard in our hearts and protect us from the anxieties that seek to overcome us.

Christian maturity requires a lifelong commitment. It is not merely asking Jesus into your life or

194

repenting once for all times. Second Corinthians 5: 17 (one of my favorite verses) states, "Therefore if any man be in Christ, he is a new creature: old things are passed away; behold: all things are become new." While this Scripture states that when Christ comes into your life that the old nature, emphasis on self, susceptibility to a sinful nature, has passed away; the newness of the Christian life is a beginning point and we as Christians must be tempered by suffering in order to reach a semblance of maturity. This lesson has and does require a commitment that many times gets lost in our daily lives. Let me give you an example of what I am talking about.

When I first graduated from law school and passed the bar exam, I was licensed by the state of Georgia to practice law in all the courts. At the moment that I was sworn in I could go before a judge or judges, represent clients, and charge fees for my services whether I was competent or not. When I first started practicing law, I could not have handled a class-action or probably even tried the case in front of a court without a more mature lawyer guiding me. I recall that shortly after I came to work in Atlanta, I was given the task of writing a brief in response to an appeal in the Georgia Court of Appeals. Law school taught me how to research and write briefs. My work for a law firm in New Orleans gave me the ability to make a persuasive argument concerning legal issues that were assigned to me. On the other hand, I had very little experience in formulating an argument that would be persuasive to the judges that sat on the Georgia Court of Appeals at that time. It took time for me to learn how to navigate the various courts and to prepare the case that I was assigned for trial.

It was not until I was guided by a lawyer who had been practicing for many years that I began to understand what was required in order to be persuasive to a jury. When considering the steps necessary to conduct the trial I learned that I had to prepare for each segment of the trial. Prior to getting ready for the trial, I had to master the facts of the case. To master the facts of the case I had to engage in discovery by asking appropriate questions of all the witnesses that might be called at the trial. I had to read and digest all the documents that were relevant to the issues that would be tried. In order to understand how the facts would fit into the trial I had to research the law relevant to the issues that would be presented. If I was handling a contract case, I needed to know the law regarding the formation of the contract, the terms of the contract, if and how the contract had been breached by one party or the other, and what damages could be claimed as a result of the breach. Once I understood the facts and the law then I had to organize those facts and the law in such a way that I could present those facts in a coherent manner to the jury and persuade the judge that there were legal authorities favorable to my client.

Some lawyers organize their case around a three ringed notebook. When I started trying cases on my own, I found it easier to organize my trial presentation in a box with folders for each segment of the trial. The first issues that would come up in the trial were usually motions concerning evidence and legal issues that should be excluded by the court. These motions are referred to as motions in limine and require that the court make rulings on whether certain evidence is admissible and whether certain arguments will be allowed before the start of the trial. I had a folder with briefs and legal arguments that I was prepared to make at the start of the trial.

Secondly, I had a folder with a written set of questions that I use for jury selection. Some say that jury selection is the most important part of any trial. I had read several books on how to handle jury selection and incorporated questions in my folder that I would use during the voir dire. The third section of my trial box contained my opening statement to the jury. In that trial folder I set out in sustained form the issues that I believed the jury should consider along with a summary of the evidence that I would present in support of my position on those issues.

Fourthly, I had a folder for each witness in the order of their appearance before the jury. In each witness's folder I had the documents or other physical evidence that I would have that witness identify and testify about. I also had a folder for each piece of evidence with a list so that I could keep track of whether that particular piece of evidence had been admitted or had been excluded by the court. There was a section in my box that contained legal arguments that I anticipated that might come up during the trial. If I was able to have a mini brief on an evidentiary matter in hand and present it to the judge while he or she was considering the evidentiary issue I would often impress the judge and therefore usually have the judge on my side of that particular issue.

In my box were outlines for the closing arguments that I was going to make. In advance I would practice making those arguments. Often, I would practice my speeches to my wives who sometimes grew weary of hearing me go on and on.

After all the evidence was in the judge would have to consider a charge to the jury that set out the legal issues and the law that applied to those issues. Lawyers are required to submit their jury charges to the court prior to the trial of the case and after the evidence is presented the court will conduct a charge conference in which the judge will tell the lawyers how he will charge the jury. Once the court decides on how he/she will charge the jury then the lawyer must quickly decide how he is going to incorporate the judge's charge into his closing statement.

I learned that if I prepared my closing argument first, so that the rest of the organization for trial would naturally build to the conclusion that I was seeking. Of course, building a case from the conclusion is not always possible and often requires that the final argument be modified once all the evidence is gathered and admitted during the trial. However, starting from the back end of the trial allows you to organize facts, testimony and documentary evidence in such a way that it flows to the ultimate conclusion that you are looking to accomplish. Much thought had to be given to the presentation of the amount of damages that were being sought. Especially in a personal injury case, the proper presentations of the amounts of the damages are critical. Sometimes even if you win the case on liability, but do not get an amount of money that was necessary to compensate your clients for the injuries that he or she suffered, the whole trial will result in a very unsatisfactory result.

Lastly, I took time to prepare a verdict form that I would submit to the court. The verdict form especially in a complex case requires the jury to answer a series of questions either in the affirmative or negatively depending upon the issue that was submitted to them. The sequence of the questions had to lead the jury in the right direction so that they could make the right decision concerning the amounts of money that were necessary in order to compensate my client. After the final arguments were made, and the judge had charged the jury with the applicable law, the jury would be sent to the jury room and the lawyers would review the physical evidence that had been admitted making sure that everything was there to send out to the jury room for the jury's consideration.

The jury had been selected, opening statements had been made, witnesses had testified, documents and other physical evidence had been identified and admitted, closing arguments had been made and the court had charged the jury with the applicable law, the jury began its deliberation; it was then and only then that I would begin to question in my mind whether I had been persuasive. I wondered whether I had parried the arguments of my opponent and I wondered what the jury was considering while they were debating the fate of my client and me. When the jury returned its verdict, they either affirmed my argument or rejected all the effort and preparation that I had put into my presentation. Usually, my client was just happy that the case was finished and that he or she could go on to something else whether they won or lost. As for me, I internalized the acceptance or the rejection and for days and weeks after the conclusion of the trial I either felt the euphoria of having won, or I felt the agony of defeat.

Preparing for trial and trying a large complex case can be also like engaging in spiritual warfare. Paul in Ephesians 5 tells us that we are to put on the whole armor of God. He reminds us that there is a spiritual warfare going on all around us all the time.

It is only when we are aware of the nature of the enemy and have adequately prepared for the warfare in which we are engaged (and we are engaged in a spiritual warfare) that we can hope to overcome the evil that so easily surrounds us. The apostle Peter, one of Jesus closest followers, states that the devil roams like an angry lion seeking to devour any who are unaware of his power and evil intent.

How then can we hope to overcome the devil and his minions?

THE HOLY SPIRIT'S LEADING

There are similarities between trying a case in front of a jury and living one's life in such a way that is pleasing to God. In Hebrews 12:1 it says, "Therefore, since we are surrounded by such a great cloud of witnesses, let us throw off everything that hinders and the sin that so easily entangles. And let us run with perseverance the race marked out for us." I like to think that there is a jury sitting in the heavenly jury box that watches each of us as we live out our lives. If we plan our closing arguments, realizing in advance what is at stake and making the right decisions concerning how the evidence will be presented by the way we live our lives we will do well. We must always remember that there is a judgment that each of us must face when we stand before God when all the evidence has been played out before that jury. Matthew 25. We must keep in mind that none of the evidence can be withheld because God knows not only our actions but also our thoughts and our intents. Too many times my life is not intentional because I don't consider the final argument that will be made when my trial on earth has come to an end.

Did I adequately consider how my presentation would be evaluated? Did I treat those around me in such a way that I wish to be treated? Matthew 7:12. Did I see someone who was hungry, thirsty, naked, sick or in jail and provide those things that would relieve their suffering? Matthew 25:35-36. Am I even capable of knowing how that I need to act and whether I have been provided with the ability to do so? In considering these questions it has become evident to me that I must rely on a greater power to provide both the ability to perceive what needs to be done and also the resources in order to accomplish the actions that need to be taken. Where does this greater power come from? To me the answer is clear. Matthew 5:3 is a potential beginning point. Jesus in what we have come to know as the Sermon on the Mount describes how his disciples should conduct their lives and respond to the presence of God. In the first Beatitude, Jesus says, "Blessed are those who are poor in spirit, for theirs is the kingdom of heaven." As we mature as Christians it becomes more and more clear that we are totally dependent on God to provide to us the means and the desire to further His kingdom. The first beatitude does not require that we take a vow of poverty but requires that we acknowledge that we are totally dependent on the grace of God to meet all of our needs. Last year after I had gone through a health crisis, a relationship crisis, a financial crisis, and even an emotional crisis, I had to take an inventory of my life and to come to the conclusion that if I was going to believe "that all things work together for good to them that love God, to them who are called according to his purpose. For those whom he for-knew he also predestined to be conformed to the image of His Son, in order that we might be the firstborn among many brethren. And those whom he predestined he also called, and those whom he called he also justified; and those whom he justified he also glorified." Romans 8:28-30. Then I had to submit to God and pray that I would not interfere in His purpose for my life. At the same time all around me people who are saying that I am foolish for not coming into conformity with the ways of the world. I have to remind myself that I am not to be conformed to the world; seeking my own pleasure, engaging in materialism, succumbing to fleshly desires, etc... While the temptations of the world are ever present, I must rely on the presence and the power of God through His Holy Spirit indwelling in my life. Paul in Philippians 4:8 tells us "Finally brothers and sisters, whatever is true, whatever is honorable, whatever is just, whatever is pure, whatever is lovely, whatever is commendable-if there is any moral excellence and if there is anything praiseworthy-dwell on these things." The power of the Holy Spirit keeps me focused and hungry and thirsty for righteousness.

When I faced multiple crises after my surgery in April 2017, I thought maybe someone was trying to get my attention and I needed to come to grips with the fact that I had suffered for a purpose. Thinking back to the time of my salvation when I was 10 years old in Hopkinsville, Kentucky I again felt Jesus' calling me to realize that my life needed to change in a dramatic way. I had been 60 years in His care, and it was time to give Jesus complete authority in every aspect of my life. It is referred to as repentance. The crisis that I was going through showed me that I was in fact "poor in spirit" and needed to become totally reliant on God's grace, because "we can cast all our cares upon Him for He cares for us." 1 Peter 5:7.

After living in Savannah for two months it was time to return to the practice of law, find a place to live, renew my relationship with Nadya, return to my Sunday school class and deal with the other issues that seemed to be overwhelming. Shortly after coming back, I was able to settle the case that I had been working on for a long time and get enough money to enable me to rent an apartment in Buckhead. The Sunday school class welcomed me back as their teacher, I set up an office where I lived and decided to stop walking with my cane. After a few months of living by myself, Nadya decided to move in with me and we made plans for a wedding. It seemed as if everything was moving in the right direction but there were still problems. My legs were not functioning nearly as well as I had hoped, and while I was able to walk without a cane (as I write this, I have had to go back to using a cane) I was always afraid of falling and my stamina limited the distance that I could effectively walk. I say all this so that you can see that even though I had made an absolute decision to become completely reliant on God's grace in my life, I had also to be patient and allow Jesus to order my life in such a way that was pleasing to Him. As I'm writing this paragraph, not everything in my life is perfect. My relationship with Nadya has problems that may or may not work to our mutual satisfaction. Our living condition is far from satisfactory. My cases continue to require lots of attention. For that matter every aspect of my life requires lots of attention.

How are we able to discern how we should conduct our lives in such a way that is pleasing to God and brings glory to God's name? I once read a book by Phillip Yancey in which he states that all human beings desire to know what it is that God wants of us. Yancey seems to think that that is a fundamental question that each of us needs to consider. How are we to know God's perfect plan for our lives? The Bible tells the story of Adam and Eve and in that story, God spoke directly to them and made clear His plans for their lives. When they disobeyed, God took away the one- on- one communication. Later, God appeared in person or in dreams to many of the other patriarchs of the Jewish religion. Notably God spoke to Abraham in a dream and that was considered it as a matter of righteousness when Abraham acted on God's instructions and relocated to a land that God had showed to him. God appeared to Joseph in a dream and allow Joseph to interpret Pharaoh's dreams. God spoke to Moses in a burning bush and directed Joshua on how to take possession of the promise land. God spoke to prophets in the Old Testament to warn Israel of the destruction that would follow when they failed to follow the commandments and took advantage of poor people.

Finally, God sent Jesus into the world to tell and show mankind about the very nature of God and what God expected of each of us. The clear message of Jesus is to repent, keep His commandments, and do onto others as we would have them do unto us. Is the message of Jesus something that we are capable of understanding and doing? In my Sunday school class we often have a debate about whether there are absolute principles (commands of Jesus) that we are capable of knowing. Some take the position that all of the commandments given to us by God require interpretation and depend upon the situation in which we find ourselves. In other words, God's commandments are subject to relevant conditions and can be applied differently depending upon the circumstances that appear at the time. Others of us believe that God's commandments are true for every situation and are absolute prerequisites for living a Christian life. In my way of thinking, it is completely necessary to know God's commandments and to have complete faith that those commandments can be understood and accomplished.

What is the source of ascertaining God's direction for each of our lives? In what ways does God speak to us today? Because there are so many sources that attempt to interpret God's commandments how are we capable of discerning God's voice? This is not to say that there is a given formula for discerning God's will. Actually, each of us must work out our own salvation as we mature.

I believe that the first step in determining whether we are following God's will is to recognize that we are dependent on God for each of our daily needs. My mother and my father prayed, on a daily basis, recognizing their dependency on God. When I was younger and active in trying cases I believed that God handled all the big stuff but left the details of our daily lives to our own devices. As I matured, I saw God at work not only in major decisions but also in the minutia of my daily life. After all, if I am in Jesus and Jesus is in me, He knows everything I am doing and will direct my path, if I will allow Him that liberty. It is hard for us to surrender each and every aspect of our lives to the will of God. Once we recognize our total dependence (poverty of spirit) we must then consider how to come before God with our requests and our needs.

One key element of coming before God is to recognize our need for repentance. I believe it is not enough to say that I am sorry. Years ago, I saw a sitcom episode on The Bob Newhart Show, in which the chambermaid Stephanie had done something to hurt the feelings of the maintenance man played by Tom Post. Stephanie was quick to say, "Sorry, sorry, sorry". But it was not until she realized how hurt the Tom Post character was that she could really learn to say in a heartfelt way that she was sorry. The same is true with us. It is not until we recognize how hurt God is by our sinful nature that we can truly say to God that we are sorry for our sinful lives and hope to restore a right relationship. King David in Psalm 57 after he had committed adultery and murder wrote, "create in me a clean heart oh God and renew a right spirit within me." It is not until we see God as the only possible source of cleaning the wickedness from our hearts that we will be able to truly seek His will in our life. After all Jesus paid the ultimate price for our sinful nature by submitting himself to Calvary's cross.

It is important also to humbly ask God to attune our hearts and minds to our proper response to the constant problems we face. Each of us should desire to be in total control of not only our actions but also our emotions. We all get angry and at times it is right to have an indignation regarding injustice wherever we see it. When I was in the third or fourth grade and Hopkinsville, Kentucky, when it was still safe to walk to and from school, my friends and me would take a regular route from our school through a very moderate neighborhood. There was a boy; his name was Tim, who would walk along the same route. Tim was not like us, he was a loner, dressed in substandard clothes, and seemed to be a little effeminate. Often the other boys would spit on him, call him names and throw rocks at him. My heart was hurt. I recall at least on several occasions in which I defended Tim when the other boys were attacking him. I do not know why I felt that way; I just knew that it was not right. Maybe I could have done more but it made me angry to see Tim treated in such a manner.

On the other hand, sometimes it is too easy to get angry over nothing. When I played baseball, I would become indignant when the umpire did not call balls and strikes the way I felt he should. There is a fine line between righteous indignation and anger because we do not get our way. Also, there are times when we may be morally right, but we express our indignation in such a way that is hurtful. Jesus was confronted by a group of Pharisees who had caught a woman in the act of adultery. They brought that woman to Jesus in order to test Jesus before they stoned her to death. The law required that these "righteous" men perform the letter of the law. Jesus's response was that the one who is without sin should cast the first stone. One by one the men who had brought the woman, caught in adultery, dropped their stones and walked away. Jesus, left alone with a woman, asked, "Where are your accusers". Jesus then said that He too did not condemn her and told her to go away and sin no more. John 7:53-8:11. In that case Jesus met the Pharisees righteous indignation with kindness that showed that He was aware of this woman's sin but was not willing to exact the penalty that the Pharisees would have imposed. When are we safe to act with righteous indignation and when is it better to show kindness even in the face of the letter of the law? We must seek that self-control that allows us to know the difference.

What other attitude do we need to exhibit in order for us to discern God's will in our lives? In the Lord's Prayer Jesus asks our Heavenly Father to "forgive us our trespasses, as we forgive those who trespass against us." If we are going to act as Christ's followers, we must be merciful. That proposition would seem to be self-evident; however, when I am driving down the road and somebody cuts me off or they fail to get out of the way, I am not very merciful in my reaction to that situation. When I was old enough to go to the movies on a Saturday morning by myself, I would often see the weekly serial.

Sometimes it was *Lash Leroux* (a Western for those of you not as old as I am) and sometimes it was *Flash Gordon*. Flash Gordon's nemesis was the evil Ming the Merciless. How cruel old Ming was. He was so cruel that he even sacrificed his beautiful daughter in order to maintain his control and power in his universe. Flash, even after he had thwarted Ming's plans to conquer earth, would have shown mercy to the Merciless if he would have accepted it. Jesus tells us that in order for us to receive mercy we must be willing to be merciful.

As a student of the law, I spent many hours in the library and in research. These days law libraries have become obsolete because everything needed to perform the research necessary to understand any given legal point is online. In order to do what is necessary, in order to understand the law on any given subject, it is necessary to thoroughly research the issue from both sides in order to come to the right conclusion. In order to understand God's will in our lives, we must understand that God is so righteous that we must diligently seek his righteousness. Jesus says that it is not enough to be satisfied with a cursory observation of God's righteousness. We are to seek God's righteousness as if our lives depend on finding the right answers. How do we come to understand what is necessary in order to desperately seek God's will in our lives?

I have never tried a case in which my client was accused of murder and the state is seeking the death penalty. I would imagine that whether or not such a client was guilty, that I would be compelled to pull out all stops in order to defend that client. That situation while requiring a diligent effort to understand the law and the facts does not approach the diligence that is necessary in order to understand God's righteousness. We all stand accused, we are all guilty, it is only by God's grace that we can avoid the death penalty. It is only by an absolute and all out pursuit of the knowledge and presence of God in our lives that we can find a blessing. When we leave no stone unturned and are completely consumed with a desire to know God that we find peace. Interestingly, pursuing God's righteousness does not necessarily lead us to a complete knowledge. Job never really understood why he had to endure the suffering that came upon him. When he questioned God, God did not fully answer. Evidently it is not important that we come to an ultimate conclusion regarding God's purpose in our lives, but it is necessary that we constantly pursue to be right with God.

In order to discern God's will, we must seek God with a proper motive. We must always examine ourselves in such a way that we eliminate any impurity in our search for God's will. William Barkley in *The Daily Study Bible* says (the Gospel of Matthew, volume 1 page 101) that we are all susceptible of impure motives in our relationships; especially our relationship with God. Barkley says it is like attempting to purge an army of those who are unfit for the coming battle. We are all susceptible to impure motives when we are seeking to fully understand God's will in our lives. Are we seeking God for the purpose of feeling ourselves to be superior even to other believers? Do we give to the church to be self-content? When I teach my Sunday school lesson and feel like I have adequately prepared and presented the Bible verses in a clear and compelling manner, do I feel self-righteous and therefore did I present the gospel with an impure heart? Paul talks about being able to lay all things aside and focusing on the goal of the knowledge of God as a runner in a race going all out in order to complete and win the gold medal. Proper self-examination, a true assessment of my motivations, is a never-ending process, but if we are truly seeking God's will in our life it is necessary to conduct that survey continuously.

In order to ascertain God's will in our lives we must do what is right with each other. In Matthew 25, Jesus says that we will all stand before God's throne and answer as to how we have treated those around us. Jesus gives a blessing to those who have seen the needs of others and acted in such a way as to show kindness, look out for other's needs, and seek to comfort those who are either sick or in trouble. It is essential for us to treat everyone that we encounter as God's creation and act in an appropriate and loving manner. If we ignore, belittle, look down our noses, or God forbid persecute anyone we will never be able to see God or ever discern how God wishes us to act in this life.

It is in these attitudes towards God and in relationship to each other that we undertake to follow Christ and to become more than merely observers of the presence of God. In the book of James, Jesus's brother says that we are not to be listeners of God's word because in doing so we would be fooling ourselves. We must do God's word in order to claim even an ability to come close to the righteousness that is necessary for us to enter into His kingdom. James 1:22. Anyone that believes that we can come close to God without a diligent and hard-fought purpose has not considered the Gospel in a complete manner. An athlete cannot effectively compete without disciplining his body, mind, and will in order to achieve success on the playing field. Likewise, Christians should not be satisfied without the proper devotion to finding the eternal truth of how we are to honor God and serve men during this life. I often ask myself is it possible to truly know what God wants of me. It is more likely than not that I will never truly find everything that I need to know about what God wants me to do in this life. It is my duty, however, to always seek, to always ask, to knock on every door in order to find the exact place in His kingdom that He has set out for me.

Yes, I was saved when I was 10 years old and felt God's call on my life. I grew to become healthy and strong. Along the way God's hand was ever present as a protector and provider. When my first child was born, I took on the responsibility of a father and started to come to grips with how I had to measure out an unconditional love to my son (and daughter). God always meted out unconditional love to me. In return God requires my unconditional love to Him and to everyone that finds their way into my life. After I had suffered a crisis that manifested itself physically, emotionally and spiritually, the truth of complete repentance presented itself to me. After 60 years of accepting, seeking, studying, teaching and even working to help those around me I still needed to completely surrender so that I can receive a fuller measure of God's grace.

I still struggle; I fail to control my anger and even improper desires. I pray daily that God will forgive me, fill me with His Spirit and make me more than a conqueror. In the name of Jesus I pray, Amen.

Acknowledgments

There were and still are many influences that have contributed to the writing of this book. I would like to thank those individuals that I have worked with who encouraged me to sit down and put some of the experiences that I have had on paper. It would be a monumental task to name all of those who have contributed to this work. However, I would like to thank the members of the Sunday school classes that I have taught for the past 40 plus years. Those class members from Second Baptist Church of College Park, Georgia; Briarcliff Baptist Church in Atlanta; First Baptist Church of Decatur Georgia; Peachtree Baptist Church of Atlanta; and Glendale Baptist Church in Glen, Mississippi. They are the long-suffering men and women who allowed me to teach their Sunday school classes and encouraged me to study and teach the Bible as I was influenced by the Holy Spirit. On many occasions it was only as a result of my prayer that the Holy Spirit would lead me in any particular lesson that gave me a confidence that the Spirit of God was present and engaging me and the class as we studied the scriptures together.

Others were also instrumental in encouraging me to write these pages. Doctor Daniel Vestal, who was my pastor at Peachtree Baptist read an early draft of this book and encouraged me to pursue publication. Doctor Peter Reha Jones, who had been my pastor at First Baptist of Decatur was also encouraging and instrumental in the study of the Sermon on the Mount (Matthew 5- 7) that has greatly influenced me in my understanding of those words spoken by Jesus. Without their encouragement it is unlikely that I would have been able to write these pages.

I would also like to thank John Mrosek a colleague and friend who also read an early draft of this book and encouraged me to go forward with the publication. John and I had become friends after we tried a case against each other in Newnan Georgia. After that time of competition in the legal arena we have collaborated on a few other cases. When John read an earlier draft, he indicated that the story was compelling enough to go forward. Additionally, I would like to thank Richard Green, another colleague in the practice of law, who patiently listened to my stories and told me that one day I should write a book.

Lastly, I would like to thank my family who have patiently allowed me to spend time and effort in the writing of this book.

CPSIA information can be obtained
at www.ICGtesting.com
Printed in the USA
LVHW050248170422
716164LV00002B/5

9 781735 619248